The
Glad Tidings

by E. J. Waggoner

Revised by Robert J. Wieland

CFI Book Division
Gordonsville, Tennessee

Published by CFI Book Division

P.O. Box 159, Gordonsville, Tennessee 38563

ISBN-10: 0-9975122-0-2
ISBN-13: 978-0-9975122-0-5

Printed in the United States of America

By carefully examining just one book of the Bible, E. J. Waggoner settles vital questions about the character of God and the eternality of His law; the importance of humanity's free will; the illogicalness of sin, and God's free gift to ensure our escape from sin's bondage. Waggoner caught the spirit of the Letter to the Galatians as few, if any, modern commentators have done. In various editions, this book has kindled fires of personal revival throughout the globe, including Australia, Africa, and North and South America. It will soon be released in Italian.

From the Publisher

CONTENTS

FOREWORD

Almost by accident I discovered reposing in a private library this rare out-of-print copy of *The Glad Tidings* by E. J. Waggoner. I knew nothing of the author, yet I felt my heart strangely warmed as I read it. I knew I had crossed a frontier by chancing upon a truly great book. Fearing I might never see another copy, I obtained permission to drag my old typewriter up to the library where I copied the most thrilling passages.

Until I found this book, what had troubled me in Galatians was the apparently irreconcilable conflict between law and faith. I knew Paul clearly upheld the law of God as "holy, and just, and good." But in Galatians he seemed to contradict himself. Apparent discrepancies and contradictions embarrassed me. Most commentaries on Galatians I found either dry or frankly antinomian. Galatians was beyond my depth, and I could not induce within myself those feelings of devotion for Christ that Paul so obviously knew. With Galatians so perplexing, how could I ever learn to "glory" in the cross as he did?

Ever since my first acquaintance with this book I have dreamed of having some small part in giving it to others, but there were obstacles. Waggoner often used the old *English Revised Version* (1881); most modern readers would not have access to it. I have substituted the *Revised Standard Version*, which usually agrees with the old *Revised Version*. Again, Waggoner's syntax was occasionally difficult. Though his writing was unusually clear and succinct for the nineteenth century, some redundancy has been eliminated without affecting the thought or emphasis of the original. Certain other passages not vital to the basic teachings of righteousness by faith have been deleted. Every care has been taken to preserve Waggoner's original message of righteousness by faith exactly as he taught it in the years of his prime. I am delighted to offer to the modern reader a treasure that I trust will prove as effective in enriching his life as it has mine.

Robert J. Wieland

INTRODUCTION

It is quite common, in writing upon any book in the Bible, to spend some time on an "introduction." But it is better to introduce the reader at once to the study of the book, and then he will soon learn, if diligent and faithful, all that it reveals concerning itself. We learn more of a man by talking with him than by hearing somebody talk about him. So we will proceed at once to the study of Paul's letter to the Galatians.

If all would study the Bible as prayerfully and as conscientiously as they ought, giving earnest heed to every word and receiving it as coming directly from God, there would be no need of any other religious book. Whatever is written should be for the purpose of calling attention more directly to the words of Scripture. Whatever substitutes any man's opinions for the Bible, so that by it people are led to rest content without any further study of the Bible itself, is worse than useless.

May God grant that this little aid to the study of the word may make every reader better acquainted with all Scripture, which is able to make him wise unto salvation.

E. J. Waggoner

CHAPTER 1

The Real Gospel: A Revelation of Jesus Christ

¹ **Paul, an apostle,—not from men, nor through man, but through Jesus Christ and God the Father, who raised him from the dead—² and all the brethren who are with me,**
To the churches of Galatia:
³ **Grace to you and peace from God the Father, and our Lord Jesus Christ, ⁴ who gave Himself for our sins to deliver us from the present evil age, according to the will of God and our Father: ⁵ to whom be the glory forever and ever. Amen.**

The first five verses form a greeting which contains the whole gospel. If there were no other portion of Scripture accessible, this contains sufficient to save the world. If we would study this small portion as diligently and prize it as highly as if there were no more, we should find our faith and hope and love infinitely strengthened. In reading it, let the Galatians sink out of sight, and let each one consider it the voice of God, through His apostle, speaking to him today.

An "apostle" is one who is sent. His confidence is in proportion to the authority of the one who sends him and to his confidence in that authority and power, "He whom God has sent utters the words of God." John 3:34. Thus it was with Paul. He spoke with authority, and the words which he spoke were the commandments of God.

See 1 Corinthians 14:37. In reading this letter or any other in the Bible, we need make no allowance for the writer's personal peculiarities and prejudices. Each writer retains his own individuality, since God chooses different men to do different work. But it is God's Word in all.

Not only the apostles, but everyone in the church is commissioned to "speak as the oracles of God." 1 Peter 4:11, KJV. All who are in Christ are new creatures, having been reconciled to God by Jesus Christ; and all who have been reconciled are given the word and ministry of reconciliation, so that they are ambassadors for Christ, as though God by them, even as by Christ, were pleading with men to be reconciled to Himself. See 2 Corinthians 5:17-20. This fact should help prevent discouragement and fear on the part of those who speak God's message. Ambassadors of earthly governments have authority according to the power of the king or ruler whom they represent. But Christians represent the King of kings and Lord of lords.

All gospel teaching is based upon the deity of Christ. The apostles and prophets were so fully imbued with this truth that it appears everywhere in their writings. Jesus Christ is "the image of the invisible God." Colossians 1:15. "He reflects the glory of God and bears the very stamp of His nature." Hebrews 1:3. He was in the beginning with God and was God before the world was. John 1:1; 17:5. "He is before all things, and in Him all things hold together." Colossians 1:17.

"Jesus Christ and God the Father, who raised Him from the dead" are associated on equal terms. "I and the Father are One." John 10:30. They both sit upon one throne. Hebrews 1:3; Revelation 3:21. The counsel of peace is between them both. Zechariah 6:12, 13, KJV. Jesus was the son of God all His life, although He was of the seed of David according to the flesh; but it was by the resurrection from the dead, accomplished by the power of the Spirit of holiness, that His Sonship was demonstrated to all. Romans 1:3, 4. This letter has the same authority as Paul's apostleship.

"Grace to you and peace from God the Father"—this is the word of the Lord and therefore means more than man's word. The Lord does not deal in empty compliments. His word creates, and here we have the form of the creative word.

God said, "'Let there be light'; and there was light." So here,

"Let there be grace and peace to you," and so it is. God has sent grace and peace, bringing righteousness and salvation to all men—even to you, whoever you are, and to me. When you read this third verse, do not read it as a sort of complimentary phrase or mere passing salutation, but as the creative word that brings to you personally all the blessings of the peace of God. It is to us the same word that Jesus spoke to the woman: "Your sins are forgiven." "Go in peace." Luke 7:48, 50.

This grace and peace come from Christ, "who gave Himself for our sins." "Unto every one of us is given grace according to the measure of the gift of Christ." Ephesians 4:7, KJV. But this grace is "the grace that is in Christ Jesus." 2 Timothy 2:1. Therefore we know that Christ Himself is given to every one of us. The fact that men live is an evidence that Christ has been given to them, for Christ is the "life," and the "life" is "the light of men." This life-light "enlightens every man." John 14:6; 1:4, 9. In Christ "all things hold together" (Colossians 1:17), and thus it is that since God "did not spare His own Son, but gave Him up for us all," He cannot do otherwise than with Him freely "give us all things." Romans 8:32. "His divine power has granted to us all things that pertain to life and godliness." 2 Peter 1:3.

The whole universe is given to us in Christ, and the fullness of the power that is in it is ours for the overcoming of sin. God counts each soul as of as much value as all creation. Christ has by grace tasted death for every man, so that every man in the world has received the "inexpressible gift." Hebrews 2:9; 2 Corinthians 9:15. "The grace of God, and the gift by grace, which is by one Man, Jesus Christ, hath abounded unto many," even to all; for "as by the offense of one judgment came upon all men to condemnation; even so by the righteousness of One the free gift came upon all men unto justification of life." Romans 5:15, 18, KJV.

Christ is given to every man. Therefore each person gets the whole of Him. The love of God embraces the whole world, but it also singles out each individual. A mother's love is not divided among her children, so that each one receives only a third, a fourth, or a fifth of it; each child is the object of all her affection. How much more so with the God whose love is more perfect than any mother's! Isaiah 49:15. Christ is the light of the world, the Sun of Righteousness. But light is not divided among a crowd of people. If a room full of people be brilliantly lighted, each individual gets the benefit of all the light, just as much as though he were alone in the room. So the life of Christ lights every man that comes into the world. In every believing heart Christ dwells in His fullness. Sow a seed in the ground and you get many seeds, each one having as much life as the original one sown.

Christ Has Bought Us

How often we hear someone say, "I am so sinful that I am afraid the Lord will not accept me!" Even some who have long professed to be Christians often mournfully wish that they could be sure of their acceptance with God. But the Lord has given no reason for any such doubts. Our acceptance is forever settled. Christ has bought us and has paid the price.

Why does a man go to the shop and buy an article? He wants it. If he has paid the price for it, having examined it so he knows what he is buying, does the merchant worry that he will not accept it? If the merchant does not deliver the goods, the buyer will ask, "Why have you not given me what belongs to me?" It is not a matter of indifference to Jesus whether we yield ourselves to Him or not. He longs with an infinite yearning for the souls He has purchased with His own blood. "The Son of man came to seek and to save the lost." Luke 19:10. God has "chosen us in Him [Christ] before the foundation of the world," and so "He hath made us accepted in the Beloved." Ephesians 1:4, 6, KJV.

Why did Christ give Himself for our sins? "To deliver us from the present evil age."

A certain man, it is said, was known for his violent temper. He would frequently become very angry, but laid the blame on the exasperating people he lived with. Nobody, he declared, could do right among such people. So he resolved to "leave the world" and become a hermit.

He chose a cave in the forest for his home, far from any other human habitation. In the morning he took his jug to a spring to get water for his meal. The rock was moss-grown and the continual flow of water had made it slippery. As he set the jug down under the stream, it slid away. He put it back, and again it was driven away. Two or three times this was repeated, each time with increasing energy.

Finally the hermit's patience was exhausted. Exclaiming, "I'll see if you'll not stay!" He picked the vessel up and set it down with such vehemence that it was broken to pieces. There was nobody to blame but himself, and he had the good sense to see that it was not the world around him but the world inside of him that made him sin.

Wherever we go, we carry the world ("this present evil age") with us. We have it in our hearts—a heavy, crushing load. We find that when we would do good, "evil is present" with us. Romans 7:21, KJV. It is present always, "this present evil age," until, goaded to despair, we cry out, "O wretched man that I am! who shall deliver me from the body of this death?" Verse 24.

Even Christ found great temptations in the desert, far from human habitations. All these things teach us that monks and hermits are not in God's plan. God's people are the salt of the earth; and salt must be mingled with that which is to be preserved.

"Deliverance" is ours. Christ was sent "to open the blind eyes, to bring out the prisoners from the prison, and them that sit in darkness out of the prison house." Isaiah 42:7, KJV. Accordingly He cries out to the captives, "Liberty!" To them that are bound He proclaims that the prison doors are "open." Isaiah 61:1. To all the prisoners He says, "Come forth." Isaiah 49:9. Each one may say if he will, "O Lord, I am Thy servant, ... the son of Thy handmaid. Thou hast loosed my bonds." Psalm 116:16.

The thing is true whether we believe it or not. We are the Lord's servants, though we may stubbornly refuse to serve. He has bought us; and having bought us, He has broken every bond that hindered us from serving Him. If we but believe, we have the victory that has overcome the world. 1 John 5:4; John 16:33. The message to us is that our "warfare is ended" and our "iniquity is pardoned." Isaiah 40:2.

> "My sin—oh, the bliss of the glorious thought!
> My sin, not in part, but the whole,
> Is nailed to His cross, and I bear it no more,
> Praise the Lord, praise the Lord, O my soul!"

The Will of God

All this deliverance is "according to the will of our God and Father." The will of God is our sanctification. 1 Thessalonians 4:3. He wills that *all* men should be saved and come to the knowledge of the truth. 1 Timothy 2:4. And He "accomplishes all things according to the counsel of His will." Ephesians 1:11. "Do you mean to teach universal salvation?" someone may ask. We mean to teach just what the Word of God teaches—that "the grace of God hath appeared, bringing salvation to all men." Titus 2:11, RV. God has wrought out salvation for every man, *and has given it to him;* but the majority spurn it and throw it away. The judgment will reveal the fact that full salvation was given to every man and that the lost have deliberately thrown away their birthright possession.

The will of God is therefore something to rejoice in and not something to be merely endured. Even though it involves suffering, it is for our good and is designed to work "for us an eternal weight of glory beyond all comparison." Romans 8:28; 2 Corinthians 4:17. We can say with Christ, "I delight to do Thy will, O My God." Psalm 40:8.

Here is the comfort of knowing the will of God. He wills our deliverance from the bondage of sin; therefore we can pray with the utmost confidence and with thanksgiving, for "this is the confidence that we have in Him, that, if we ask anything according to His will, He heareth us; and if we know that He hear us, whatsoever we ask, we know that we have the petitions that we desired of Him." 1 John 5:14, 15, KJV.

To God be the glory for this deliverance! All glory is His, whether men acknowledge it or not. To give Him the glory is not to impart anything to Him, but to recognize a fact. We give Him the glory by acknowledging that His is the power. "It is He that hath made us, and not we ourselves." Psalm 100:3, KJV.

Power and glory are related, as we learn from the Lord's prayer. When Jesus by His power had turned water into wine, we are told that in this miracle He "manifested His glory." John 2:11. So when we say that to God is the glory, we acknowledge that power is all from Him. We do not save ourselves, for we are "without strength." If we confess that all glory belongs to God, we shall not be indulging in vainglorious imaginations or boastings.

The last proclamation of "the everlasting gospel," which announces that the hour of God's judgment has come, has for its burden, "Fear God and give Him glory." Revelation 14:7. Thus the letter to the Galatians, which ascribes to Him "the glory," is the setting forth of the everlasting gospel. It is emphatically a message for the last days. If we study it and heed it, we may help to hasten the time when "the earth will be filled with the knowledge of the glory of the Lord, as the waters cover the sea." Habakkuk 2:14.

⁶ I am astonished that you are so quickly deserting Him who called you in the grace of Christ and turning to a different gospel—⁷ not that there is another gospel, but there are some who trouble you and want to pervert the gospel of Christ. ⁸ But even if we, or an angel from heaven, should preach to you a gospel contrary to that which we preached to you, let him be accursed. ⁹ As we have said before, so now I say again, If any one is preaching to you a gospel contrary to that which you received, let him be accursed.

The apostle now plunges into the midst of his subject. His spirit seems to be on fire, and seizing his pen he writes as only one can write who feels upon his heart the burden of souls about to rush to destruction.

Paul's brethren were in mortal danger, and he could not waste time on compliments. He must get at once to his subject in as clear and direct terms as possible.

Who "calls" men? "God is faithful, by whom you were called into the fellowship of His Son, Jesus Christ our Lord." 1 Corinthians 1:9, "The God of all grace, who has called you to His eternal glory in Christ." 1 Peter 5:10. "The promise is to you and to your children and to all that are far off, everyone whom the Lord our God calls to Him." Acts 2:39. Those that are near and those that are far off—this includes all that are in the world. Therefore *God calls everybody.* (Not all come, however!)

But did Paul refer to himself as the one who had called the Galatian brethren and from whom they were now removing? A little thought should convince us how impossible that would be. Paul himself said that the apostasy would be the result of men's seeking to draw away disciples after themselves (Acts 20:30); he, as the servant of Christ, would be the last man to draw people to himself. Although God uses human agents such as Paul, it is nevertheless God who calls. We are only ambassadors for Christ. It is God beseeching men by us to be reconciled to Himself. There may be many mouths, but there is only one voice.

Separating From God

Since the Galatian brethren were separating from Him that had called them, and as God is the one who graciously calls men, it is evident that they were deserting the Lord. It is a small matter to join or desert men, but a matter of vital importance to be joined to God.

Many seem to think that if they are only "members in good standing" in this or that church, they are secure. But the only thing worth considering is, Am I joined to the Lord and walking in His truth? If one is joined to the Lord, he will very soon find his place among God's people; for those who are not His people will not tolerate a zealous follower of God among them very long. When Barnabas went to Antioch, he exhorted the brethren that with purpose of heart they should "remain faithful to the Lord." See Acts 11:22, 23. That was all that was necessary. If we do that, we shall certainly find the Lord's own people very soon.

Those who were deserting the Lord were "without God in the world" just to the extent that they were removing from Him. But those who are in that condition are Gentiles, or heathen. Ephesians 2:11, 12. Therefore the Galatian brethren were relapsing into heathenism. It could not be otherwise; for whenever a Christian loses his hold on the Lord, he inevitably drops back into the old life from which he had been saved. No more helpless condition can exist in the world than to be without God.

"Another Gospel"

How can there be "another gospel"? The true gospel is "the power of God for salvation to everyone who has faith." Romans 1:16. God Himself is the power, and deserting Him means deserting the gospel of Christ.

Nothing can be called a gospel unless it professes to give salvation. That which professes to offer nothing but death could not be called a "gospel," which means "good news" or "joyful news." A promise of death does not answer that description. In order for any false doctrine to pass as the gospel, it must pretend to be the way of life; otherwise it could not deceive people. The Galatians were being seduced from God by something that promised them life and salvation but by a power other than that of God. This other gospel was only a human gospel. A sham is nothing. A mask is not a man. So this other gospel to which the Galatian brethren were being enticed was only a perverted gospel, a counterfeit, a sham, and no real gospel at all.

The question would follow, Which is the true gospel? Is it the one that Paul preached? or the one the others preached?

Just as Jesus Christ is to us the power of God and there is no other name than that of Jesus whereby salvation can be obtained, so there can be only one true gospel. That which Paul preached to the Galatians and to the Corinthians as well, "Jesus Christ and Him crucified," was the gospel preached by Enoch, Noah, Abraham, Moses, and Isaiah. "To Him give all the prophets witness, that through His name whosoever believeth in Him shall receive remission of sins." Acts 10:43, KJV.

If any man, or even an angel from heaven, should preach contrary to what Paul and the prophets preached, he would bring himself under a curse. There are not two standards of right and wrong. That which will bring a curse today would have produced the same five thousand years ago. The way of salvation has been exactly the same in every age. The gospel preached to Abraham (Galatians 3:8) was genuine, angels being sent to him; and the ancient prophets preached the same gospel. 1 Peter 1:11, 12. If the gospel preached by them of old had been different from that preached by Paul, even they would have been "accursed."

But why should one be "accursed" for preaching a different gospel? Because he is the means of fastening others in the curse, by leading them to trust for their salvation in that which is nothing. Since the Galatians were deserting God, they were trusting to supposed human power, their own power, for salvation. But no man can save another (Psalm 49:7, 8); and "cursed is the man who trusts in man and makes flesh his arm, whose heart turns away from the Lord." Jeremiah 17:5. The one who leads men into the curse must of course himself be accursed.

"Cursed be he who misleads a blind man on the road." Deuteronomy 27:18. If this be so of the one who causes a physically blind man to stumble, how much more must it apply to one who causes a soul to stumble to its eternal ruin! To delude the people with a false hope of salvation—what could possibly be more fatal? It is to lead people to build their house over the bottomless pit.

An Angel From Heaven

But is there any possibility that an "angel from heaven" could preach any other than the one true gospel? Most assuredly, although it would not be an angel recently come from heaven. "Satan himself is transformed into an angel of light. Therefore it is no great thing if his ministers also be transformed as the ministers of righteousness." 2 Corinthians 1:14, 15, KJV. It is they who come professing to be the spirits of the dead and to bring messages fresh from the realms beyond the grave. They preach invariably "another gospel" than the gospel of Jesus Christ. Beware of them. "Beloved, do not believe every spirit, but test the spirits to see whether they are of God." 1 John 4:1. "To the law and to the testimony: if they speak not according to this word, it is because there is no light in them." Isaiah 8:20, KJV. No one need be deceived, so long as he has God's Word. In fact, it is impossible to be deceived while one holds to the Word of God.

¹⁰ Am I now seeking the favor of men, or of God? Or am I trying to please men? If I were still pleasing men, I should not be a servant of Christ.

In the first three centuries the church became leavened with paganism, and in spite of reformations, much of paganism still remains. This was the result of trying to seek "the favor of men." The bishops thought they could gain influence over the heathen by relaxing some of the strictness of the principles of the gospel, which they did. The result was the corruption of the church.

Self-love is always at the bottom of efforts to conciliate and please men. The bishops desired (often perhaps without being conscious of it) to draw away disciples after themselves. Acts 20:30. In order to gain the favor of the people they had to compromise and pervert the truth.

This was being done in Galatia. Men were perverting the gospel. But Paul was seeking to please God and not men. He was the servant of God, and God was the only one he needed to please. This principle is true in every kind of service. Employees who try only to please men will not be faithful employees, for they will do good work only where it can be seen and will slight any task that cannot come under the eye of the inspectors. So Paul exhorts: "Servants, obey in all things your masters according to the flesh; not with eye-service, as men-pleasers … : whatever ye do, do it heartily, as to the Lord." Colossians 3:22-24, KJV.

There is a tendency to dull the edge of truth, lest we should lose the favor of some wealthy or influential person. How many have stifled conviction, fearing the loss of money or position! Let every one of us remember, "If I were still pleasing men, I should not be a servant of Christ." But this does not mean we shall be stern and uncourteous. It does not mean that we willingly offend any. God is kind to the unthankful and the unholy. We are to be soul winners and so must have a winning manner. We must exhibit only the attractiveness of the loving, crucified One.

¹¹ For I would have you know, brethren, that the gospel which was preached by me is not man's gospel. ¹² For I did not receive it from man, nor was I taught it, but it came through a revelation of Jesus Christ.

The gospel is divine, not human. In the first verse the apostle says he was not sent by man, and he is not anxious to please man, but only Christ. Now it is made very clear that the message he bore was wholly from heaven. By birth and education he was opposed to the gospel, and when he was converted it was by a voice from heaven. The Lord Himself appeared to him in the way as he was breathing threatening and slaughter against the saints of God. Acts 9:1-22.

There are no two persons whose experience in conversion is the same, yet the general principles are the same in all. In effect, every person must be converted just as Paul was. The experience will seldom be so striking; but if it is genuine, it must be a revelation from heaven as surely as Paul's was. "All thy children shall be taught of the Lord." Isaiah 54:13, KJV. "Every man therefore that hath heard, and hath learned of the Father, cometh unto Me." John 6:45, KJV. "The anointing which ye have received of Him abideth in you, and ye need not that any man teach you." 1 John 2:27, KJV.

Do not make the mistake of supposing that this does away with the necessity for any human agency in the gospel. God has set apostles, prophets, teachers and others, in the church (1 Corinthians 12:28); it is the Spirit of God that works in all these. No matter by whom anyone first hears the truth, he is to receive it as coming directly from heaven. The Holy Spirit enables those who wish to do God's will to tell what is truth as soon as they see or hear it; and they accept it, not on the authority of the man through whom it came to them, but on the authority of the God of truth. We may be as sure of the truth which we hold and teach as the apostle Paul was.

But whenever anybody cites the name of some highly esteemed scholar to justify his belief, or to give it more weight with some person whom he would convince, you may be sure that he himself does not know the truth of what he professes. It may be the truth, but he does not know for himself that it is truth. It is everybody's privilege to know the truth. John 8:31, 32. And when one holds a truth directly from God, ten thousand times ten thousand great names in its favor do not add a feather's weight to its authority, nor is his confidence in the least shaken if every great man on earth should oppose it.

The Revelation of Jesus Christ

Note that Paul's message is not simply a revelation from Jesus Christ, but is "the revelation *of* Jesus Christ." It is not simply that Christ told Paul something, but Christ revealed Himself to Paul. The mystery of the gospel is Christ *in* the believer, the hope of glory. Colossians 1:25-27. Only so can the truth of God be known and be made known. Christ does not stand afar off and lay down right principles for us to follow; but He impresses Himself upon us, takes possession of us as we yield ourselves to Him, and makes manifest His life in our mortal flesh. Without this life shining forth, there can be no preaching of the gospel. Jesus was revealed *in* Paul in order that Paul might preach Him among the heathen. He was not to preach *about* Christ, but to preach Christ Himself. "What we preach is not ourselves, but Christ Jesus as Lord." 2 Corinthians 4:5.

God is waiting and anxious to reveal Christ in every man. We read of men "who by their wickedness suppress the truth," and that "what can be known about God is plain to them," even as in everything that God has made His "eternal power and deity" are clearly seen (Romans 1:18-20). Christ is the truth (John 14:6) and also the power of God (1 Corinthians 1:24), and He *is* God (John 1:1). Therefore Christ Himself is the truth that men "suppress." He is the divine Word of God, given to all men, that they may do it. See Deuteronomy 30:14; Romans 10:6-8.

But in many people Christ is so "suppressed" that it is difficult to discern Him. The very fact that they live is proof that Christ loves them and would save them. But He must patiently wait the time when they will receive the Word and thus His perfect life be manifested in them.

This may take place in "whosoever will" *now*, no matter how sinful and degraded he may be. It pleases God to do it; cease then to resist.

¹³ **For you have heard of my former life in Judaism, how I persecuted the church of God violently and tried to destroy it;** ¹⁴ **and I advanced in Judaism beyond many of my own age among my people, so extremely zealous was I for the traditions of my fathers.** ¹⁵ **But when He who had set me apart before I was born, and had called me through His grace,** ¹⁶ **was pleased to reveal His Son to me, in order that I might preach Him among the Gentiles, I did not confer with flesh and blood,** ¹⁷ **nor did I go up to Jerusalem to those who were apostles before me, but I went away into Arabia; and again I returned to Damascus.**

Why did Paul persecute the church so violently and try to destroy it? He tells us that he was simply zealous for the traditions of his fathers! Before Agrippa he said: "I verily thought with myself, that I ought to do many things contrary to the name of Jesus of Nazareth. Which thing I also did in Jerusalem: and many of the saints did I shut up in prison, having received authority from the chief priests; and when they were put to death, I gave my voice against them. And I punished them oft in every synagogue, and compelled them to blaspheme; and being exceedingly mad against them, I persecuted them even unto strange cities." Acts 26:9-11, KJV.

All this mad zeal for the traditions of his fathers Paul thought was "being zealous for God." Acts 22:3.

It seems almost incredible that anyone professing to worship the true God could have such false ideas of Him as to suppose that He is pleased with that kind of service; yet this bitter and relentless persecutor of Christians could say years afterward, "I have lived before God in all good conscience up to this day." Acts 23:1. Although trying to silence the growing conviction that would force itself upon him as he witnessed the patience of the Christians and heard their dying testimonies to the truth, Saul was not willfully stifling his conscience. On the contrary, he was striving to preserve a good conscience! So deeply had he been taught the Pharisaic traditions that he felt sure these inconvenient convictions must be the suggestions of an evil spirit which he was in duty bound to suppress. So the convictions of the Spirit of God for a time only led him to redouble his zeal against the Christians. Of all persons in the world, Saul, the self-righteous Pharisee, had no bias in favor of Christianity. He was indeed a rising young man, on whom the rulers of the Jews looked with pride and hope, believing that he would contribute much to the restoration of the Jewish nation and religion to their former greatness. There had been a promising future before Saul from a worldly point of view. But what things were gain to him, those he counted loss for Christ, for whose sake he suffered the loss of all things. Philippians 3:7, 8.

But Judaism was not the religion of God and Jesus Christ. It was human tradition. Many make a great mistake in considering "Judaism" the religion of the Old Testament. The Old Testament no more teaches Judaism than the New Testament teaches Romanism. The religion of the Old Testament is the religion of Jesus Christ.

When Paul was "in Judaism" he did not believe the Old Testament, which he read and listened to daily, because he did not understand it; if he had, he would have readily believed on Christ. "For they that dwell at Jerusalem, and their rulers, because they knew Him not, nor yet the voices of the prophets which are read every Sabbath day, they have fulfilled them in condemning Him." Acts 13:27, KJV.

The traditions of the fathers led to breaking the commandments of God. Matthew 15:3. God said of the Jewish people: "This people draweth nigh unto Me with their mouth, and honoreth Me with their lips; but their heart is far from Me. But in vain do they worship Me, teaching for doctrines the commandments of men." Verses 8, 9, KJV. Jesus had no word of condemnation for Moses and his writings. He said to the Jews, "If you believed Moses, you would believe Me; for he wrote of Me." John 5:46. Everything which the scribes read and commanded from his writings was to be followed; but the example of the readers was to be shunned, for they did not obey the Scriptures. Christ said of them, "They bind heavy burdens, hard to bear, and lay them on men's shoulders; but they themselves will not move them with their finger." Matthew 23:4.

These were not the commandments of God, for "His commandments are not burdensome" (1 John 5:3); and the burdens were not of Christ, for His "burden is light" (Matthew 11:30). These Judaizing teachers were not presenting the Bible or any part of it to the new converts, or trying to get them to follow the Scriptures written by Moses. Far from it! They were leading them away from the Bible and substituting for its teaching the commandments of men. This was what aroused the spirit of Paul.

On his way to Damascus, "breathing out threatenings and slaughter," Saul was proceeding with full authority to seize and drag to prison all Christians, both men and women, when he was suddenly arrested, not by human hands, but by the overpowering glory of the Lord. Three days afterward the Lord said to Ananias, when sending him to give Saul his sight, "He is a chosen instrument of Mine to carry My name before the Gentiles." Acts 9:15.

How long before this had Saul been chosen to be the messenger of the Lord? He himself tells us, "Before I was born." He is not the first one of whom we read that from birth he was chosen to his lifework. Recall the case of Samson. Judges 13. John the Baptist was named and his character and lifework were described months before he was born. The Lord said to Jeremiah: "Before I formed thee in the belly I knew thee; and before thou camest forth out of the womb I sanctified thee, and I ordained thee a prophet unto the nations." Jeremiah 1:5, KJV. The heathen king Cyrus was named more than a hundred years before he was born, and his part in the work of God was laid out before him. Isaiah 44:28; 45:1-4.

These are not isolated cases. It is as true of all men as it was of the Thessalonians that God chose them "from the beginning to be saved, through sanctification by the Spirit and belief in the truth." 2 Thessalonians 2:13. It rests with everyone to make that calling and election sure. And He who "desires all men to be saved, and to come to the knowledge of the truth" (1 Timothy 2:3, 4), has also appointed to each man his own work (Mark 13:34). So He who leaves not Himself without witness even in the inanimate creation would have man, His highest earthly creation, willingly give such witness to Him as can be given only by human intelligence.

All men are chosen to be witnesses for God, and to each is his labor appointed. All through life the Spirit is striving with every man, to induce him to allow himself to be used for the work to which God has called him. Only the judgment day will reveal what wonderful opportunities men have recklessly flung away. Saul, the violent persecutor, became the mighty apostle. Who can imagine how much good might have been done by other men whose great power over their fellows has been exerted only for evil, if these also had yielded to the influence of the Holy Spirit? Not everyone can be a Paul; but the truth that each one according to the ability God has given him is chosen and called of God to witness for Him will give to life a new meaning.

What a wonderful, a joyous, and yet a solemn thought, as we

see men moving about, that to each one of them God has given a work of his own to do! They are all servants of the Most High God, each one assigned to special service. We should be extremely careful not to hinder anyone in the slightest degree from doing his Heaven-appointed task.

Since it is God who gives to every man his work, each is to receive his orders from God and not from men. Therefore we should beware of dictating to men concerning their duty. The Lord can make it plain to them as well as to us; and if they will not hear Him, they will not be likely to hear us even if we could direct them in the right way. "It is not in man who walks to direct his steps" (Jeremiah 10:23), much less to direct the steps of some other man.

Conferring With Flesh and Blood

Not till three years after his conversion did Paul go up to Jerusalem. Then he stayed only fifteen days and saw only two of the apostles. The brethren were afraid of him and would not at first believe he was a disciple. Thus it is evident that he did not receive the gospel from any man.

There is much to learn from Paul's not conferring with flesh and blood. To be sure, he had no need to, since he had the Lord's own word. But such a course as his is by no means common. For instance, a man reads a thing in the Bible and then must ask some other man's opinion before he dare believe it. If none of his friends believe it, he is fearful of accepting it. If his pastor, or some commentary, explains the text away, then away it goes. "Flesh and blood" gain the day against the Spirit and the Word.

It may be that the commandment is so plain that there is no reasonable excuse for asking anybody what it means. Then the question is, "Can I afford to do it? Will it not cost too much sacrifice?" The most dangerous "flesh and blood" one can confer with is one's own. It is not enough to be independent of others; in matters of truth one must be independent of one's self. "Trust in the Lord with all thine heart; and lean not unto thine own understanding." Proverbs 3:5, KJV.

A pope is one who presumes to occupy the place in counsel which rightfully belongs to God alone. The man who makes himself pope by following his own counsel is just as bad as the man who dictates to another, and he is more likely to be led astray than is the man who follows some pope other than himself. If one is to follow a pope at all, it would be more consistent to accept the pope of Rome, because he has had more experience in popery than any other. But none is necessary, since we have the Word of God. When God speaks, the part of wisdom is to obey at once without taking counsel even of one's own heart. The Lord's name is "Counselor" (Isaiah 9:6), and He is "wonderful" in counsel. Hear Him!

"Immediately"

Paul lost no time. He thought he was serving God when he was persecuting the church, and the moment he found out his mistake he turned about. When he saw Jesus of Nazareth, he recognized Him as his Lord and immediately cried out, "Lord, what shall I do?" He was ready to be set to work in the right way, and that immediately. Would that everybody might truthfully say, "I hasten and do not delay to keep Thy commandments." Psalm 119:60. "I will run in the way of Thy commandments when Thou enlargest my understanding." Verse 32.

Paul says that Christ was revealed in him that he might preach Him among the Gentiles, that is, the heathen. In 1 Corinthians 12:2, KJV, we read, "Ye know that ye were Gentiles, carried away unto these dumb idols, even as ye were led." Take notice that the Corinthians *were* "Gentiles"; they ceased to be such on becoming Christians!

"God first visited the Gentiles, to take out of them a people for His name." Acts 15:14. And James referred to the believers in Antioch and elsewhere as "those of the Gentiles who turn to God." Verse 19. God's people are taken out from among the Gentiles, but on being taken out, they cease to be Gentiles. Abraham, the father of Israel, was taken from among the heathen (Joshua 24:2) even as Israel are taken from among the Gentiles. Thus it is that "all Israel will be saved" by the coming in of the fullness of the Gentiles. Romans 11:25, 26.

The Lord was as anxious for the conversion of the Gentiles three thousand years ago as He is today. The gospel was preached to them before the first coming of Christ as well as it was afterward. By many agencies the Lord made Himself known among all nations. Jeremiah was specially chosen as the prophet to the Gentiles or heathen. "Before thou camest forth out of the womb I sanctified thee, and I ordained thee a prophet unto the nations." Jeremiah 1:5, KJV. The Hebrew word from which the word "nations" is translated is the very same that is regularly translated "heathen." Let no one say that God ever confined His truth to any one people, whether Jew or Gentile. "There is no difference between the Jews and the Greek; for the same Lord over all is rich unto all that call upon Him." Romans 10:12, KJV.

The New Convert Preaching

As soon as Paul was converted, "immediately he proclaimed Jesus." Acts 9:20. Was it not marvelous that he should at once be able to preach so powerfully? Indeed, it is marvelous that any man can preach Christ. But do not suppose that Paul got his knowledge instantaneously, without any study. Remember that he had all his life been a diligent student of the Scriptures. Paul, who had more advancement than any other of his age, was as familiar with the words of the Bible as a bright schoolboy is with the multiplication table. But his mind was blinded by the traditions of the fathers, which had been drilled into him at the same time. The blindness which came upon him when the light shown round him on the way to Damascus was but a picture of the blindness of his mind; and the seeming scales that fell from his eyes when Ananias spoke to him indicated the shining forth of the Word within him, and the scattering of the darkness of tradition.

We may be sure that since preaching was his lifework, he did not spend all the months he was in Arabia in study and contemplation. He had been so severe a persecutor, and had received so richly of God's grace, that he counted all the time lost in which he couldn't reveal that grace to others, feeling, "Woe to me if I do not preach the gospel!" 1 Corinthians 9:16. He preached in the synagogues in Damascus as soon as he was converted, before he went to Arabia. So it is but natural to conclude that he preached the gospel to the Arabs. He could preach there without the opposition that he always received when among the Jews, and therefore his labors would not so much interfere with his meditation on the new worlds that had just opened before him.

18 Then after three years I went up to Jerusalem to visit Cephas, and remained with him fifteen days. 19 But I saw none of the other apostles except James the Lord's brother. 20 (In what I am writing to you, before God, I do not lie!) 21 Then I went into the regions of Syria and Cilicia. 22 And I was still not known by sight to the churches of Christ in Judea; 23 they only heard it said, "He who once persecuted us is now preaching

the faith he once tried to destroy." [24] And they glorified God because of me.

Let no one look on any opposer of the gospel as incorrigible. Those who make opposition are to be instructed with meekness, for who knows but that God will give them repentance to the acknowledgement of the truth?

One might have said of Paul, "He has had the light as clearly as any man can have it. He has had every opportunity; he has not only heard the inspired testimony of Stephen, but he has heard the dying confessions of many martyrs. He is a hardened wretch from whom it is useless to expect any good." Yet that same Paul became the greatest preacher of the gospel even as he had been the most bitter persecutor.

Is there a malignant opposer of the truth? Do not strive with him, and do not reproach him. Let him have all the bitterness and strife to himself, while you hold yourself to the word of God and to prayer. It may not be long until God who is now blasphemed will be glorified in him.

Glorifying God

How different Paul's case was from that of those to whom he said, "The name of God is blasphemed among the Gentiles because of you." Romans 2:24. Everyone who professes to be a follower of God should be a means of bringing glory to His name, yet many cause it to be blasphemed. How can we cause His name to be glorified? "Let your light so shine before men, that they may see your good works, and give glory to your Father who is in heaven." Matthew 5:16.

CHAPTER 2

Life by the Faith of Christ

Many are reading this little book not out of curiosity to see what another person thinks about the letter to the Galatians, but for actual help in understanding that much-discussed portion of Scripture. With each one of you I wish to hold a little personal talk before we proceed farther.

Every portion of Scripture is connected with every other portion; as soon as we learn one thing thoroughly, making it a part of ourselves, it joins us and aids us in the search for *more* knowledge, just as each morsel of food that we eat and assimilate assists us in our labor for our daily bread. If, therefore, we proceed in the right way with the study of the epistle to the Galatians, we shall have opened a wide door to the *whole* Bible.

The way to knowledge is so simple that many despise it. It is a royal road, open to all: "My son, if you *receive* My words and *treasure up* My commandments with you, making your ear *attentive* to wisdom and *inclining your heart* to understanding; yes, if you *cry out* for insight and ... *seek* it like silver and *search* for it as for hidden treasures; then you will understand. ... For the Lord gives wisdom." Proverbs 2:1-6.

God appeared to Solomon in a dream and promised to give him wisdom; but it was not by idle dreaming that the wisdom came. Solomon did not go to sleep and wake up to find himself the wisest man that ever lived. He longed for knowledge so much that he did indeed dream of it by night, but *he worked for it by day.*

If you would understand the Word of God, study it. No man on earth can give you his knowledge. Another may tell you so that it need not take you as long as it took him; he may direct you how and where to work; but whatever anyone really knows he must acquire for himself. When you have traveled over a road a thousand times, you know every turn in it and can see the whole way in your mind. So after you have thought through a portion of Scripture time after time, you will at last be able to see the whole of it, and every separate statement in it at a single glance. And when you can do that, you will see in it what no other on earth can tell you.

¹ Then after fourteen years I went up again to Jerusalem with Barnabas, taking Titus along with me. ² I went up by revelation; and I laid before them (but privately before those who were of repute) the gospel which I preach among the Gentiles, lest somehow I should be running or had run in vain. ³ But even Titus, who was with me, was not compelled to be circumcised, though he was a Greek.

"After fourteen years," following the natural course of the narrative, means fourteen years after the visit of Galatians 1:18, which was three years after Paul's conversion. This visit therefore was seventeen years after his conversion, or about A.D. 51, which coincides with the conference in Jerusalem recorded in Acts 15. It is with that conference and the things that led to it and grew out of it that the second chapter of Galatians deals.

In the first chapter we are told that some were troubling the brethren by perverting the gospel of Christ, presenting a false gospel and pretending that it was the true one. In Acts 15:1 we read that "some men came down from Judea and were teaching the brethren, 'Unless you are circumcised according to the custom of Moses, you cannot be saved.'" This was the "different gospel," which was not "another," since there is only one, which was being palmed off on the brethren as the true gospel.

Paul and Barnabas would not give any place to the new preaching, but withstood it "that the truth of the gospel might be preserved for you." Galatians 2:5. The apostles had "no small dissension and debate with them." Acts 15:2. The controversy was between the real gospel and a counterfeit.

A Denial of Christ

A glance at the experience of the church at Antioch to which this new gospel was brought will show that it did in the most direct manner deny the power of Christ to save.

The gospel was first brought to them by brethren scattered by the persecution after the death of Stephen. These brethren came to Antioch "preaching the Lord Jesus. And the hand of the Lord was with them, and a great number that believed turned to the Lord." Acts 11:20, 21. Included in the church were prophets and teachers; and as they ministered unto the Lord and fasted, the Holy Spirit impressed them to "set apart" Barnabas and Saul to the work to which He had called them. Acts 13:1-3. The church there had had much experience in the things of God. They were acquainted with the Lord and with the voice of the Holy Spirit.

And now after all this, these men said, "Unless you are circumcised according to the custom of Moses, you cannot be saved." That was as much as to say, All your faith in Christ, and all the witness of the Spirit, are nothing without the sign of circumcision. The sign of circumcision without faith was exalted above faith in Christ without any outward sign. The new "gospel" was a most direct assault upon the true gospel and a clear denial of Christ.

It is no wonder that Paul styles those who "sneaked in" (Danish version) with this teaching as "false brethren":

⁴ But because of false brethren secretly brought in, who slipped in to spy out our freedom which we have in Christ Jesus, that they might bring us into bondage—⁵ to them we did not yield submission even for a moment, that the truth of the gospel might be preserved for you.

In chapter one Paul had said that these false brethren "trouble you and want to pervert the gospel of Christ." Verse 7. In their letter to the churches, the apostles and elders said of those men, "We have heard that some persons from us have troubled you with words, unsettling your minds, although we gave them no instructions." Acts 15:24.

There have been many such since that time. So vicious was this work that the apostle said of anyone doing it, "Let him be accursed." Galatians 1:8, 9. "These preachers were deliberately seeking to undermine the gospel of Christ and thus to destroy the believers.

These false brethren had said, "Unless you are circumcised according to the custom of Moses, you cannot be saved." (Literally, you have not *power* to be saved.) They made salvation only a human thing, resulting solely from human power. They did not know what circumcision really is: "He is not a Jew, which is one outwardly, neither is that circumcision, which is outward in the flesh: but he is a Jew, which is one inwardly; and circumcision is that of the heart, in the spirit, and not in the letter; whose praise is not of men, but of God." Romans 2:28, 29, KJV.

There was a time, after Abraham believed God, when he listened to the voice of Sarah instead of to God and sought to fulfill the promises of God by the power of his own flesh. See Genesis 16. The result was a failure—a bondservant instead of an heir. Then God appeared to him again, exhorting him to walk before Him with singleness of heart, and repeating His covenant. As a reminder of his failure and of the fact that "the flesh profiteth nothing," Abraham received the sign of circumcision, a cutting off of the flesh. This was to show that since in the flesh "dwelleth no good thing," the promises of God can be realized only by putting away the sins of the flesh. "For we are the true circumcision, who worship God in spirit, and glory in Christ Jesus, and put no confidence in the flesh." Philippians 3:3.

Abraham was therefore *really* circumcised when he received the Spirit through faith in God. "And he received the *sign* of circumcision, a *seal* of the righteousness of the faith which he had yet being uncircumcised." Romans 4:11, KJV. Outward circumcision was never anything more than a sign of the real circumcision *of the heart*. When this was absent, the sign was a fraud; but when the real circumcision was there, the sign could be dispensed with. Abraham is "the father of all them that *believe*, though they be not circumcised." Romans 4:11, KJV. The "false brethren" were substituting the empty sign for the reality. With them the shell of the nut without the kernel counted for more than the kernel without the shell.

Jesus said, "It is the Spirit that quickeneth; the flesh profiteth nothing: the words that I speak unto you, they are Spirit, and they are life." John 6:63, KJV. The people of Antioch and Galatia had trusted in Christ for salvation; now there were some who sought to induce them to trust in the flesh. They did not tell them that they were at liberty to sin. Oh, no; they told them that they must keep the law! Yet they must do it themselves; they must make themselves righteous without Jesus Christ. Circumcision stood for keeping the law. But the *real* circumcision was the law written in the heart by the Spirit; and these "false brethren" wished the believers to trust in the *outward* form of circumcision as a substitute for the Spirit's work. The thing which was given as a sign of righteousness by faith became only a sign of self-righteousness. The "false brethren" would have them circumcised for righteousness and salvation; but "man believes with his heart and so is justified." Romans 10:10. And "whatever does not proceed from faith [believing with the heart] is sin." Romans 14:23. Therefore, all the efforts of men to keep the law of God by their own power, no matter how earnest and sincere they may be, can never result in anything but imperfection—sin.

When the question came up in Jerusalem, Peter said to those who would have been justified by their own works instead of by faith in Christ, "Now therefore why tempt ye God, to put a yoke upon the neck of the disciples, which neither our fathers nor we were able to bear?" Acts 15:10, KJV.

This yoke was a yoke of bondage, as is shown by Paul's words that the "false brethren" slipped in "to spy out our freedom which we have in Christ Jesus, that they might bring us into bondage." Galatians 2:4. Christ gives freedom from sin. His life is "the perfect law of liberty." "Through the law comes knowledge of sin" (Romans 3:20), but not freedom from sin. "The law is holy, and the commandment is holy and just and good" (Romans 7:12) because it gives the knowledge of sin by condemning it. It is a signpost which points out the way, but it does not carry us. It can tell us that we are out of the way, but Jesus Christ alone can make us walk in it, for He *is* the way. Sin is bondage. Only those who keep the commandments of God are at liberty (Psalm 119:45); and the commandments can be kept only by faith in Christ (Romans 8:3, 4).

Therefore whoever induces people to trust in the law for righteousness without Christ simply puts a yoke upon them and fastens them in bondage. When a man convicted by the law is cast into prison, he cannot be delivered from his chains by the law which holds him there. But that is no fault of the law. Just because it is a good law, it cannot say that a guilty man is innocent.

The apostle says that he withstood the false teaching now misleading the Galatian brethren so "that the truth of the gospel might be preserved for you." It is self-evident that this letter contains nothing else but the gospel in the most forcible form of expression. Many have misunderstood it and derived no personal gain from it because they thought it was only a contribution to the "strivings about the law" against which Paul himself had warned the brethren.

⁶ And from those who were reputed to be something (what they were makes no difference to me; God shows no partiality)—those, I say, who were of repute added nothing to me; ⁷ but on the contrary, when they saw that I had been entrusted with the gospel to the uncircumcised, just as Peter had been entrusted with the gospel to the circumcised.

Acts says that it was determined at Antioch that Paul and Barnabas and some others should go up to Jerusalem about this matter. But Paul says that he went up "by revelation." Galatians 2:2. He did not go up simply on their recommendation, but the same Spirit moved both him and them. He did not go up to learn the truth of the gospel, but to maintain it; not to find out what the gospel really is, but to communicate what he had preached among the heathen. Those who were important in the conference imparted nothing to him. He had not received the gospel from any man, and he did not need to have any man's testimony that it was genuine. When God has spoken, an endorsement by man is an impertinence. The Lord knew that the brethren in Jerusalem needed his testimony, and the new converts needed to know that those whom God sent spoke the words of God, and therefore all spoke the same thing. They needed the assurance that as they had turned from "many gods" to serve the one God, truth is also one, and that there is but one gospel for all men.

The Gospel Is Not Magic

There is nothing in this world that can confer grace and righteousness upon men, and there is nothing in the world that any man can do that will bring salvation. The gospel is the power of *God* unto salvation, not the power of man. Any teaching that leads men to trust in any object, whether it be an image, a picture, or anything else, or to trust for salvation in any work or effort of their own, even though that effort be directed toward the most praise-worthy object, is a perversion of the truth of the gospel—a false gospel. There are in the church of Christ no "sacraments" that by some sort of magical working confer special grace on the receiver; but there are deeds that a man who believes in the Lord Jesus Christ, and who is thereby justified and saved, may do as an *expression* of his faith. "By grace are ye saved through faith; and that not of yourselves: it is the gift of God: not of works, lest any man should boast. For we are His workmanship, created in Christ Jesus unto good works, which God hath before prepared that we should walk in them." Ephesians 2:8-10, KJV, margin. This is "the truth of the gospel," and it was for this that Paul stood. It is the gospel for all time.

No Monopoly of Truth

There is no man or body of men on earth that has a monopoly of truth—a corner, so to speak, so that whoever wishes it must come to them. Truth is independent of men. Truth is of God; for Christ, who is the shining of His glory and the very impress of His substance (Hebrews 1:3), is the truth (John 14:6). Whoever gets the truth must get it from God and not from any man, just as Paul received the gospel. God may and does use men as instruments or channels, but He alone is the Giver. Neither names nor numbers have anything to do with determining what is truth. It is no more mighty nor to be accepted more readily when presented by ten thousand princes than when maintained by a single humble labor-ing man. And there is no more presumptive evidence that ten thousand men have the truth than that one has it. Every man on earth may be the possessor of just as much of the truth as he is willing to use, and no more. See John 7:17; 12:35, 36. He who would act the pope, thinking to hold a monopoly of the truth and compel people to come to him for it, giving it out here and withholding it there, loses all the truth that he ever had (if he ever really had any). Truth and popery cannot exist together; no pope, or man with a popish disposition, has the truth. As soon as a man receives the truth, he ceases to be a pope. If the pope of Rome should become converted and be a disciple of Christ, that very hour he would vacate the papal seat.

Just as there is no man who has a monopoly of truth, so there are no places to which men must necessarily go in order to find it.

The brethren in Antioch did not need to go to Jerusalem to learn the truth or to find out if what they had was the genuine article. The fact that truth was first proclaimed in a certain place does not prove that it can be found only there, or that it can be found there at all. In fact, the last places in the world to go to with the expectation of finding or learning truth are the cities where the gospel was preached in the first centuries after Christ, as Jerusalem, Antioch, Rome, or Alexandria.

The papacy arose in part in this way. It was assumed that the places where the apostles, or some of them, had preached must have the truth in its purity and that all men must take it from there. It was also assumed that the people of a city must know more of it than the people in the country or in a village. So, from all bishops being on an equality as at the beginning, it soon came to pass that the "country bishops" (*chorepiscopoi*) were rated as secondary to those who officiated in the cities. When that spirit crept in, the next step was necessarily a strife among the city bishops to see which one should be greatest; and the unholy struggle went on until Rome gained the coveted place of power.

But Jesus was born in Bethlehem, a place that was "little among the thousands of Judah" (Micah 5:2, KJV), and nearly all His life lived in a little town of so poor repute that a man in whom there was no guile said, "Can anything good come out of Nazareth?" See John 1:45-47. Afterward Jesus took up His abode in the wealthy city of Capernaum, but He was always known as "Jesus of Nazareth." It is no farther to heaven from the smallest village or even the smallest lonely cabin on the plain than it is from the largest city or the bishop's palace. And God, "the high and lofty One who inhabits eternity, whose name is Holy," dwells with him that is of a contrite and humble spirit. Isaiah 57:15.

Appearances Are Nothing

God looks at what a man is, not at what he is reputed to be. What he is reputed to be depends largely on the eyes of those who look at him; what he is demonstrates the measure of the power and wisdom of God that is in him. God does not set any store upon official position. It is not position that gives authority, but authority that gives the real position. Many a humble, poor man on earth, with never an official title to his name, has occupied a position really higher and of greater authority than that of all the kings of the earth. Authority is the unfettered presence of God in the soul.

8 (for He who worked through Peter for the mission to the circumcised worked through me also for the Gentiles),

The Word of God is living and active. Hebrews 4:12. Whatever activity there is in the work of the gospel, if there is any work done, is all of God. Jesus "went about doing good," "for God was with Him." Acts 10:38. He Himself said, "I can do nothing on My own authority." John 5:30. "The Father who dwells in Me, *He* does the works." John 14:10. So Peter spoke of Him as "a Man approved of God" "by miracles and wonders and signs, which *God* did by Him." Acts 2:22, KJV. The disciple is not greater than his Lord. Paul and Barnabas, therefore, at the meeting in Jerusalem, told "what signs and wonders *God* had done through them among the Gentiles." Acts 15:12. Paul declared that he labored to "present every man mature *in Christ*," "striving with all the energy which He mightily inspires within me." Colossians 1:28, 29. This same power the humblest believer may possess, "for it is God which worketh in you both to will and to do of His good pleasure." Philippians 2:13, KJV. The name of Jesus is Immanuel, "God with us." *God* with Jesus caused Him to go about doing good. He is unchangeable; therefore, if we truly have Jesus, God with us, we likewise will go about doing good.

9 and when they perceived the grace that was given to me, James and Cephas and John, who were reputed to be pillars, gave to me and Barnabas the right hand of fellowship, that we should go to the Gentiles and they to the circumcised; 10 only they would have us remember the poor, which very thing I was eager to do.

The brethren in Jerusalem showed their connection with God in that "they perceived the grace that was given to" Paul. Those who are moved by the Spirit of God will always be quick to "perceive" workings of the Spirit in others. The surest evidence that one knows nothing personally of the Spirit is that he cannot recognize His working. The other apostles had the Holy Spirit, and they "perceived" that God had chosen Paul for a special work among the Gentiles; and, although his manner of working was different from theirs, for God had given him special gifts for his special work, they freely gave to him the right hand of fellowship, only requesting that he would remember the poor among his own nation; "which very thing I was eager to do."

Perfect Unity

Remember that there was no difference of opinion among the apostles nor in the church as to what the gospel is. There were "false brethren," it is true; but inasmuch as they were false, they were no part of the church, the body of Christ, which is the truth. Many professed Christians, sincere persons, suppose that it is almost a matter of necessity that there be differences in the church. "All cannot see alike," is the common statement. So they misread Ephesians 4:13, KJV, making it seem that God has given us gifts "*till* we all come into the unity of the faith." What the Word teaches is that "*in* the unity of the faith, and of the knowledge of the Son of God," we all come "unto a perfect man, unto the measure of the stature of the fullness of Christ." There is only "one faith" (verse 5), the faith of Jesus, as there is only one Lord; and those who have not that faith must necessarily be out of Christ.

Truth is the Word of God, and the Word of God is light; nobody but a blind man ever has any trouble to see a light that shines. The fact that a man has never in his life seen any other light used at night, except that from a tallow candle, does not in the least stand in the way of his recognizing that the light from an electric lamp is light, the first moment he sees it. There are, of course, different degrees of knowledge, but never any controversy between those different degrees. All truth is one.

11 But when Cephas came to Antioch I opposed him to his face, because he stood condemned. 12 For before certain men came from James, he ate with the Gentiles; but when they came he drew back and separated himself, fearing the circumcision party. 13 And with him the rest of the Jews acted insincerely, so that even Barnabas was carried away by their insincerity.

We need not magnify nor dwell upon the mistakes of Peter or any other good man. That is not profitable for us. But we must note this overwhelming proof that Peter was never considered the "prince of the apostles," and that he never was and never considered himself to be pope. Fancy any priest, bishop, or cardinal withstanding a pope to his face in a public assembly!

But Peter made a mistake, and that upon a vital matter of doctrine, because he was not infallible. He meekly accepted the rebuke that Paul gave him like the sincere, humble Christian that he was. If there were such a thing as a human head to the church, it would evidently be Paul instead of Peter, as appears from the whole narrative. Paul was sent to the Gentiles, and Peter to the Jews; but the Jews formed only a very small portion of the church; the converts from the Gentiles soon outnumbered them, so that their presence was scarcely discernible. All these Christians were largely the fruit of Paul's labors, and they naturally looked up to him more than to the others, so that Paul could say that upon him daily came "the care of all the churches." 2 Corinthians 11:28, KJV. But infallibility is not the portion of any man, and Paul himself did not claim it. The greatest man in the church of Christ has no lordship over the weakest. Jesus said, "One is your Master, even Christ; and all ye are brethren." Matthew 23:8, KJV. And Peter admonished us, "Be subject one to another." 1 Peter 5:5, KJV.

When Peter was at the conference in Jerusalem, he told the facts how the Gentiles received the gospel through his preaching: "God who knows the heart bore witness to them, giving them the Holy Spirit just as He did to us; and He *made no distinction* between us and them, but cleansed their hearts by faith." Acts 15:8, 9. Why? Because, knowing the hearts, He knew that "all have sinned and fall short of the glory of God," so that there is no other way than for all to be "justified by His grace as a gift, through the redemption which is in Christ Jesus." Romans 3:23, 24. Yet, after having been shown this fact by the Lord—after having preached to the Gentiles, and after having witnessed the gift of the Holy Ghost to them the same as to Jewish believers; after having eaten with those Gentile converts, and faithfully defending his course; after having given a clear testimony in conference, that God made no difference between Jews and Gentiles; and even immediately after himself making no difference—Peter suddenly, as soon as "certain men" came who he thought would not approve of such freedom, began to make a difference! "He drew back and separated himself, fearing the circumcision party." This was, as Paul says, "insincerity," and was not only wrong in itself, but would confuse and mislead the disciples. It was fear, not faith, that for the moment controlled Peter.

Contrary to the Truth of the Gospel

A wave of fear seems to have passed over the Jewish believers, for "with him the rest of the Jews acted insincerely, so that even Barnabas was carried away with their insincerity." Of course, "they were not straightforward about the truth of the gospel" (verse 14);

but the mere fact of insincerity was not the whole of the offense against the truth of the gospel. Under the circumstances it was a public denial of Christ, just as much as when Peter once before through sudden fear had been guilty. We have all been too often guilty of the same sin to permit us to sit in judgment; we can only note the fact and the natural consequence as a warning to ourselves.

¹⁴ But when I saw that they were not straightforward about the truth of the gospel, I said to Cephas before them all, "If you, though a Jew, live like a Gentile and not like a Jew, how can you compel the Gentiles to live like Jews?"

See how the action of Peter and the others was a virtual though unintentional denial of Christ. There had just been a great controversy over circumcision. It was a question of justification and salvation—whether men were saved by faith alone in Christ, or by outward forms. Clear testimony had been borne that salvation is by faith alone; and now, while the controversy is still alive while the "false brethren" are still propagating their errors, these loyal brethren suddenly discriminated against the Gentile believers because they were uncircumcised. In effect they said to them, "Unless you are circumcised, you cannot be saved." Their actions said, "We also are in doubt about the power of faith in Christ alone to save men; we really believe that salvation depends on circumcision *and* the works of the law; faith in Christ is good, but there's something more to do; it is not in itself sufficient." Such a denial of the truth of the gospel Paul could not endure, and he at once struck directly at the root of the matter.

¹⁵ We ourselves, who are Jews by birth and not Gentile sinners, ¹⁶ yet who know that a man is not justified by works of the law but through faith in Jesus Christ, even we have believed in Christ Jesus, in order to be justified by faith of Christ, and not by works of the law, because by works of the law shall no one be justified.

Did Paul mean that they, being Jews, were therefore not sinners? By no means, for he immediately adds that they had believed on Jesus Christ for justification. They were merely Jewish sinners, and not Gentile sinners! Whatever things they had to boast of as Jews, all had to be counted loss for the sake of Christ. Nothing availed them anything except faith in Christ; and since this was so, it was evident that the Gentile sinners could also be saved directly by faith in Christ without going through the dead forms which had been of no service to the Jews, and which were given largely as the result of their unbelief.

"This is a faithful saying, and worthy of all acceptation, that Christ Jesus came into the world to save sinners." 1 Timothy 1:15, KJV. *All* have sinned and stand alike guilty before God; but all, of whatever race or class, *can* accept this saying, "This Man receives sinners, and eats with them." Luke 15:2. A circumcised sinner is no better than an uncircumcised one; a sinner who stands as a church member is no better than one who is outside. The sinner who has gone through the form of baptism is not better than the sinner who has never made any profession of religion. Sin is sin, and sinners are sinners, whether in the church or out. But, thank God, Christ is the sacrifice for our sins, as well as for the sins of the whole world. There is hope for the unconverted church member as well as for the sinner who has never named the name of Christ. The same gospel that is preached to the world must be preached to the church, for there is only one gospel. It serves to convert sinners in the world as well as sinners who stand as church members. And at the same time it renews those who are really in Christ.

The meaning of the word "justified" is "made righteous." The Latin word for righteousness is *justitia*. To be just is to be righteous. Then we add the termination *fy* from the Latin word, meaning "to make," and we have the exact equivalent of the simpler term, "make righteous."

In a sense we use the term "justified" of a man who has not done the wrong he is accused of doing. Such a person needs no justification, since he is already just. But since "all have sinned," no one is just or righteous before God. Therefore all need to be justified, or *made* righteous.

Now the law of God is righteousness. See Romans 7:12; 9:30, 31; Psalm 119:172, KJV. So highly did Paul appreciate the law that he believed in Christ for the righteousness which the law demands but cannot give: "For what the law could not do, in that it was weak through the flesh, God sending His own Son in the likeness of sinful flesh, and for sin, condemned sin in the flesh: that the righteousness of the law might be fulfilled in us, who walk not after the flesh, but after the Spirit." Romans 8:3, 4, KJV. The law, which declares all men to be sinners, could not justify them except by declaring that sin is not sin. And that would not be justification, but contradiction.

Shall we say, "then we will do away with the law"? Persistent lawbreakers would gladly do away with the law which declares them guilty. But the law of God cannot be abolished, for it is the life and character of God. "The law is holy, and the commandment holy, and just, and good." Romans 7:12, KJV. When we read the written law, we find in it our duty made plain. But we have not *done* it. Therefore we are guilty.

Moreover, there is not one who has strength to keep the law, for its requirements are great. While no one can be justified by the works of the law, the fault is not in the law, but in the individual. Get Christ in the heart by faith, and then the righteousness of the law will be there also. As the psalmist says, "I *delight* to do Thy will, O my God; Thy law is within my heart." Psalm 40:8. The one who would throw away the law because it will not call evil good, would also reject God because He "will by no means clear the guilty." Exodus 34:7. But God will remove the guilt, and will thus make the sinner righteous, that is, in harmony with the law.

Much is lost by not noting exactly what the Scriptures say. In the original in verse 16 we have "faith of Christ" just as in Revelation 14:12 we have "faith of Jesus." He is "the Author and Finisher of our faith." Hebrews 12:2, KJV. "Faith cometh by hearing, and hearing by the Word of God" (Romans 10:17, KJV), and Christ is the Word. God has "dealt to every man the measure of faith" (Romans 12:3, KJV) in giving Christ to every man.

There is therefore no opportunity for anyone to plead that his faith is weak. He may not have accepted and made use of the gift, but there is no such thing as "weak faith." A man may be "weak in faith," that is, may be afraid to depend on faith; but faith itself is as strong as the Word of God. Christ alone is righteous. He has overcome the world. He alone has power to do it. In Him is all the fullness of God, because the law—God Himself—is in His heart. He alone has kept and can keep the law to perfection. Therefore, only by His faith—living faith, that is, His life in us—can we be made righteous.

But this is sufficient. He is a "tried Stone." The faith which He gives to us is His own tried and approved faith, and it will not fail us in any contest. We are not exhorted to *try* to do as well as He did, or to *try* to exercise as much faith as He had, but simply to take *His* faith, and *let* it work by love, and purify the heart. It will do it!

"As many as received Him, to them gave He power to become the sons of God, even to them that believe on His name." John 1:12, KJV. That is, as many as believed on His name received Him. To believe on His name is to believe that He is the Son of God. To believe that He is the Son of God means to believe that He is come in the flesh, human flesh, our flesh. For His name is "God with us."

So believing in Christ, we are justified by the faith of Christ, since we have Him personally dwelling in us, exercising His own faith. All power in heaven and earth is in His hands. Recognizing this, we simply allow Him to exercise His own power in His own way. This He does "exceeding abundantly" by "the power that worketh in us."

¹⁷ But if, in our endeavor to be justified in Christ, we ourselves were found to be sinners, is Christ then an agent of sin? Certainly not!

Jesus Christ is "the Holy and Righteous One." Acts 3:14. "He was manifested to take away our sins; and in Him is no sin." 1 John 3:5, KJV. He not only "committed no sin" (1 Peter 2:22), but also "knew no sin" (2 Corinthians 5:21). Therefore it is impossible that any sin can come from Him. He does not impart sin. In the stream of life that flows from the heart of Christ through His wounded side there is no trace of impurity. He is not the minister of sin, that is, He does not minister sin to anybody.

If in anyone who has sought (and not only sought, but found) righteousness through Christ, there is afterward found sin, it is because the person has dammed up the stream, allowing the water to become stagnant. The Word has not been given free course so that it could be glorified. And where there is no activity, there is death. No one is to blame for this but the person himself. Let no professed Christian take counsel of his own imperfections and say that it is impossible for a Christian to live a sinless life. It is impossible for a true Christian, one who has full faith, to live any other kind of life. "How can we who died to sin still live in it?" Romans 6:2. "Whosoever is born of God doth not commit sin; for His seed remaineth in him; and he cannot sin, because he is born of God." 1 John 3:9, KJV. Therefore "abide in Him."

¹⁸ But if I build up again those things which I tore down, then I prove myself a transgressor.

If a Christian tears down or destroys his sins through Christ and then later builds those sins back up, he again becomes a lawbreaker in need of Christ.

Remember that the apostle is talking about those who have believed in Jesus Christ, and have been justified by the faith of Christ. In Romans 6:6 (KJV) Paul writes, "Our old man is crucified with Him, that the body of sin might be destroyed, that henceforth we should not serve sin."

That which is destroyed is the body of sin, and it is destroyed only by this personal presence of the life of Christ. It is destroyed in order that we may be freed from its power and may no longer need to serve it. It is destroyed for everybody, for Christ in His own flesh has abolished "the enmity," the sinner's carnal mind. Our sins, our weaknesses, were upon Him. For every soul the victory has been gained, and the enemy has been disarmed. We have only to accept the victory which Christ has won. The victory over all sin is already a reality. Our faith in it makes it real to us. The loss of faith puts us outside the reality, and the old body of sin looms up again. That which is destroyed by faith is built up again by unbelief. Remember that this destruction of the body of sin, although performed by Christ for all, is nevertheless a present, personal matter with each individual.

¹⁹ For I through the law died to the law, that I might live to God.

Many seem to fancy that "I died to the law" means the same as that the law died. Not by any means. The law must be in full force, else no one could die to it. How does a man become dead to the law? By receiving its full penalty, which is death. He is dead, but the law which put him to death is still as ready as ever to put to death another criminal. Suppose, now, that the man who was executed for gross crimes should by some miraculous power come to life again; would he not still be dead to the law? Certainly. Nothing that he had done could be mentioned to him by the law. But if he should again commit crimes, the law would again execute him, but as another man. I am raised from the death which I have suffered by the law because of my sin, and now I walk "in newness of life," a life unto God. Like Saul of old, I am by the Spirit of God "turned into another man." 1 Samuel 10:6.

²⁰ I have been crucified with Christ; it is no longer I who live, but Christ who lives in me; and the life I now live in the flesh I live by faith in the Son of God, who loved me and gave Himself for me.

But unless we are crucified with Him, His death and resurrection profit us nothing. If the cross of Christ is separated from us, and outside of us, even though it be but by so much as a moment of time and an hair breadth of space, it is to us all the same as if He were not crucified. If men would see Christ crucified, they must look upward; for the arms of the cross that was erected on Calvary reach from Paradise lost to Paradise restored, and embrace the whole world of sin. The crucifixion of Christ is not a thing of but a single day. He is "the Lamb slain from the foundation of the world." Revelation 13:8, KJV. And the pangs of Calvary will not be ended as long as a single sin or sinners exists in the universe. Even now Christ bears the sins of the whole world, for "in Him all things consist." And when at last He is obliged to cut off the irreclaimably wicked in the lake of fire, the anguish which they suffer will be no more than that which the Christ whom they have rejected suffered on the cross.

Christ bore our sins in His own body on the tree. 1 Peter 2:24. He was "made a curse for us," in that He hung on the tree. Galatians 3:13. On the cross He bore not only the weakness and sin of humanity, but also the curse of the earth. Thorns are a sign of the curse (Genesis 3:17, 18), and Christ bore the crown of thorns. Every trace of the curse is borne by Christ.

Wherever we see a fallen, sin-scarred, miserable human being, we ought to see also the Christ of God crucified for him. Christ on the cross bears all things, and the sins of that man are on Him. Because of his unbelief he may feel all the weight of the heavy burden. But if he will believe, he may be relieved of the load. Christ bears the sins of all the world on the cross. Therefore, wherever sin is found, there we may be sure is the cross of Christ.

Sin is a personal matter. It is in the heart of man. "For from within, out of the heart of men, proceed evil thoughts, adulteries, fornications, murders, thefts, covetousness, wickedness, deceit, lasciviousness, an evil eye, blasphemy, pride, foolishness: all the evil things come from within." Mark 7:21-23, KJV. "The heart is deceitful above all things, and desperately corrupt." Jeremiah 17:9. Sin is in every fiber of our being by nature. We are born in it, and our life is sin, so that sin cannot be taken from us without taking our life. What I need is freedom from my own personal sin—that sin which not only has been committed by me personally, but which dwells in the heart, the sin which constitutes all of my life.

My sin is committed by myself, in myself, and I cannot separate it from me. Shall I cast it on the Lord? Yes, that is right; but how? Can I gather it up in my hands and cast it from me, so that it will light upon Him? If I could separate it but a hair breadth from me, then I should be safe, no matter what became of it, since it would not be found in me. In that case I could dispense with Christ. For if sin were not found on me, it would make no matter to me where it was found. It would then be away from me, and I would be cleared. But nothing that I can do can save me. Therefore all my efforts to separate myself from my sins are unavailing.

Therefore whoever bears my sins must come where I am, must come into me. This is just what Christ does. Christ is the Word, and to all sinners who would excuse themselves by saying that they cannot know what God requires of them, He says, "The Word is very near you; it is in your mouth and in your heart, so that you can do it." See Deuteronomy 30:11-14. Therefore, He says, If you confess with your lips that Jesus is Lord and believe in your heart that God raised Him from the dead, you will be saved." Romans 10:9. What shall we confess about the Lord Jesus? Confess the truth, that He is near you, even in your mouth and in your heart, and believe that He is there risen from the dead. The risen Saviour is the crucified Saviour. As Christ risen is in the heart of the sinner, therefore Christ crucified is there. If it were not so, there would be no hope for any. A man may believe that Jesus was crucified two millennia ago, and may die in his sins. But he who believes that Christ is crucified and risen in him has salvation.

All any man in the world has to do in order to be saved is to believe the truth; that is, to recognize and acknowledge facts, to see things just as they actually are, and to confess them. Whoever believes that Christ is crucified in him, risen in him, and dwells in him, is saved from sin. And he will be saved as long as he holds to his belief. This is the only true confession of faith.

In the tenth chapter of Romans, as already noted, we learn that Christ by the Spirit comes to every man, "a very present help in trouble." Psalm 46:1. He comes to the sinner, in order that the sinner may have every incentive and facility for turning from sin to righteousness. He is "the way, and the truth, and the life." John 14:6. There is no other life than His. But although he comes to every man, not every man shows His righteousness, for some "suppress the truth." Romans 1:18.

Paul's inspired prayer was that we might be strengthened with might by the Spirit of God in the inner man, "that Christ may dwell in your hearts through faith," "that you may be filled with all the fullness of God." See Ephesians 3:16-19.

Christ is crucified in the sinner; for wherever there is sin and the curse, there is Christ bearing it. All that is needed now is for the sinner to be crucified with Christ, to let Christ's death be his own death, in order that the life of Jesus may be manifested in his mortal flesh. Faith in the eternal power and divinity of God, that are seen in all the things that He has made, will enable anyone to grasp this truth. The seed does not grow "unless it dies." 1 Corinthians 15:36. "Unless a grain of wheat falls into the earth and dies, it remains alone; but if it dies, it bears much fruit." John 12:24. So the one who is crucified with Christ begins at once to live as another man. "It is no longer I who live, but Christ who lives in me."

But Christ was actually crucified eighteen hundred years and more ago, was He not? Certainly. Then how can it be that my personal sins were upon Him? or how can it be that I am now crucified with Him? Well, it may be that we cannot understand the fact, but that makes no difference with the fact. When we remember that Christ is the life, even "the eternal life which was with the Father and was made manifest to us" (1 John 1:2), we may understand something of it. "In Him was life; and the life was the light of men." He is "the true Light, which lighteth every man that cometh into the world." John 1:4, 9, KJV.

Flesh and blood (that which the eyes can see) cannot reveal "the Christ, the Son of the living God." See Matthew 16:16, 17. "Eye hath not seen, nor ear heard, neither have entered into the heart of man, the things which God hath prepared for them that love Him. But God hath revealed them unto us by His Spirit." 1 Corinthians 2:9, 10, KJV. No man, no matter how well acquainted he was with the Carpenter of Nazareth, could call Him Lord but by the Holy Spirit. 1 Corinthians 12:3.

By the Spirit, His own personal presence, He can come to every man on earth and fill the heavens as well, a thing which Jesus in the flesh could not do. Therefore it was expedient for Him to go away and to send the Comforter. "He is before all things and in Him all things hold together." Colossians 1:17. Jesus of Nazareth was Christ in the flesh. The Word who was in the beginning, and whose power upholds all things, is the Christ of God. The sacrifice of Christ, so far as this world is concerned, dates from the foundation of the world. Revelation 13:8; 1 Peter 1:18-20.

The scene on Calvary was the manifestation of what has taken place as long as sin has existed, and will take place until every man is saved who is willing to be saved: Christ bearing the sins of the world. He bears them now. One act of death and resurrection was sufficient for all time, for it is eternal life that we are considering. Therefore it is not necessary for the sacrifice to be repeated. That life is for all men everywhere, so that whoever accepts it by faith has all the benefit of the entire sacrifice of Christ. By Himself He "made purification of sins." Whoever rejects the life loses the benefit of the sacrifice.

Christ lived by the Father. John 6:57. His faith in the word that God gave Him was such that He repeatedly and positively maintained that when He died He should rise again the third day. In this faith He died, saying, "Father, into Thy hands I commit My spirit." Luke 23:46. The faith that gave Him victory over death also gave Him complete victory over sin. That same faith He exercises in us when He dwells in us by faith, for He is "the same yesterday and today and forever." Hebrews 13:8.

It is not we that live, but Christ that lives in us, and uses His own faith to deliver us from the power of Satan. "What have we to do?" Let Him live in us in His own way. "Let this mind be in you, which was also in Christ Jesus." Philippians 2:5, KJV. How can we let Him? Simply by acknowledging Him, by confessing Him.

"Who loved me and gave Himself for me." How personal this is! I am the one He loved! Each soul in the world can say, "He loved me and gave Himself for me." Paul is dead, but the words he wrote are yet alive. It was true of Paul, but no more so than of every other man. They are the words the Spirit puts in our mouths, if we will but receive them. The whole gift of Christ is for each individual "me." Christ is not divided, but every soul gets the whole of Him, just the same as if there were not another person in the world. Each one gets all the light that shines. The fact that there are millions of people for the sun to shine upon does not make its light any the less for me. I get the full benefit of it. I could get no more if I were the only person in the world. So Christ gave Himself for me, the same as if I were the only sinner in the world. And the same is true of every other sinner.

When you sow a grain of wheat, you get many more grains of the same kind, each one having the same life, and just as much of it, as the original seed had. So it is with Christ, the true Seed. In dying for us, that we may also become the true seed, He gives to every one of us the whole of His life. "Thanks be to God for His inexpressible gift." 1 Corinthians 9:15.

²¹ I do not nullify the grace of God; for if justification were through the law, then Christ died to no purpose.

If we could save ourselves, Christ died for nothing, for salvation is the one thing to be gained. But we cannot save ourselves. And Christ did not die in vain. Therefore there is salvation only in Him. He is able to save all that come unto God by Him. Some must be saved, else He has died in vain. But He did not die in vain. Therefore the promise is sure: "He shall see His seed, He shall prolong His days, and the pleasure of the Lord shall prosper in His hand. He shall see of the travail of His soul, and shall be satisfied." Isaiah 53:10, 11, KJV.

"Whosoever will" may be saved. Since He did not die in vain, see to it that "ye receive not the grace of God in vain." 2 Corinthians 6:1, KJV.

CHAPTER 3

Redeemed From the Curse

The Galatians, having accepted the gospel, were led astray by false teachers who presented to them "another gospel," a counterfeit gospel, since there is but one for all time and for all men.

The counterfeit gospel was represented in these words: "Unless you are circumcised according to the custom of Moses, you cannot be saved." Now, although there is in these days no question as to whether or not a man should submit to the specific rite of circumcision in order to be saved, the question of salvation itself, whether by human works or by Christ alone, is as alive as ever.

Instead of attacking their error and combating it with hard argument, the apostle begins with an experience which illustrates the case in hand. In this narrative he shows that salvation is wholly by faith for all men alike, and not in any degree by works. As Christ tasted death for every man, so every man who is saved must have Christ's personal experience of death and resurrection and life. Christ in the flesh does what the law cannot do. Galatians 2:21; Romans 8:3, 4. But that very fact witnesses to the righteousness of the law. If the law were at fault, Christ would not fulfill its demands. He shows its righteousness by fulfilling or doing what it demands, not simply *for* us but *in* us. We do not "nullify the grace of God." If righteousness could come by the law, "then Christ died to no purpose."

But to claim that the law could be abolished, or could relax its claims and thus be of no account, is also to say that Christ is dead in vain. Let it be repeated, righteousness cannot possibly come by the law, but only by the faith of Christ. But the fact that the righteousness of the law could be attained in no other way by us than by the crucifixion and resurrection and life of Christ *in* us shows the infinite greatness and holiness of the law.

¹ O foolish Galatians! Who has bewitched you, before whose eyes Jesus Christ was publicly portrayed as crucified?

"Behold, to obey is better than sacrifice, and to hearken than the fat of rams. For rebellion is as the sin of *witchcraft*, and stubbornness is as iniquity and idolatry." 1 Samuel 15:22, 23, KJV. Stubbornness and rebellion are rejection of God. And he who rejects God puts himself under the control of evil spirits. All idolatry is devil worship. "The things which the Gentiles sacrifice, they sacrifice to devils." 1 Corinthians 10:20, KJV. There is no middle ground. Christ says, "He who is not with Me is against Me." Matthew 12:30. That is, disobedience, rejection of the Lord, is the spirit of antichrist. The Galatian brethren were, as we have already seen, departing from God; consequently, they were inevitably, although perhaps unconsciously, relapsing into idolatry.

The Safeguard Against Spiritualism

Spiritualism is only another name for ancient witchcraft and soothsaying. It is a fraud, but not the kind of fraud many people think it is. There is reality in it. It is a fraud in that while it professes to receive communications from the spirits of the dead, it has communication only with the spirits of devils, since "the dead know not anything." To be a spiritualist medium is to give one's self to the control of demons.

Now there is only one protection against this, and that is to hold fast to the Word of God. *He who lightly regards God's Word, severs himself from association with God*, and puts himself within Satan's influence. Even though a man denounce spiritualism in the strongest terms, if he does not hold to God's Word he will sooner or later be carried away by the strong false-christ delusion. Only by keeping close to the word of God can men be kept from the temptation that is coming on all the world. Revelation 3:10. "The spirit that is now at work in the sons of disobedience" (Ephesians 2:2) is the spirit of Satan, the spirit of antichrist; and the gospel of Christ, which reveals the righteousness of God (Romans 1:16, 17), is the only possible salvation from it.

Christ Crucified Before Us

Jesus was set forth before the Galatians, when Paul preached to them, as openly crucified before their eyes. So vivid was the presentation that they could actually see Christ crucified. It was not only skillful word painting on the part of Paul and imagination on the part of the Galatians. Through Paul the Holy Spirit enabled them to see Him crucified.

The experience of the Galatians in this matter cannot be peculiar to them. The cross of Christ is a present thing. The expression, "Come to the cross," is not an empty form of words, but an invitation that can be literally complied with.

Not until one has seen Christ crucified before his eyes, and can see the cross of Christ at every turn, does one know the reality of the gospel. Let those scoff who will—the fact that a blind man cannot see the sun and denies that it shines will not deter one who sees it from telling of its glory. Many there are who can testify that it is something more than a figure of speech when the apostle says that Christ was crucified before the eyes of the Galatians. They too have had the experience. God grant that this study of Galatians, before it is finished, may be the means of opening the eyes of many more!

² Let me ask you only this: Did you receive the Spirit by works of the law, or by hearing of faith?

The question, "Did you receive the Spirit by works of the law, or by hearing of faith?" admits of but one answer. It was by hearing with faith. The Spirit is given to those who believe. John 7:38, 39; Ephesians 1:13. The question also shows that the Galatians had received the Holy Spirit. There is no other way of beginning the Christian life. "No one can say 'Jesus is Lord' except by the Holy Spirit." 1 Corinthians 12:3. In the beginning the Spirit of God moved upon the face of the waters, begetting life and activity in the creation, for without the Spirit there is no motion—no life. "Not by might, nor by power, but by My Spirit, says the Lord of hosts." Zechariah 4:6. The Spirit of God alone can carry out the perfect will of God; and no works that a man can do can bring Him into the soul, any more than a dead man can manufacture the breath by which he can be made to live and move. Those to whom Paul addressed this letter had seen Christ crucified before their eyes and had accepted Him through the Spirit. Have you also seen and accepted Him?

³ Are you so foolish? Having begun with the Spirit, are you now ending with the flesh?

"Foolish" is but a feeble term for it! The man who has not power to *begin* a work, thinks he has strength to *finish* it! He who has not strength to put one foot before the other, or even to stand alone, thinks he has strength enough in himself to win a race!

Who has power to beget himself? No one. We come into this world without having begotten ourselves. We are born without strength. Therefore all the strength that ever manifests itself in us comes from another than ourselves. It is all given to us. The newborn babe is the representative of man. "A man is born into the world." All the strength that any man has of himself is found in the infant as it utters its first cry with its first breath. And even that feeble strength is not of itself.

Even so in things spiritual. "Of His own will He brought us forth by the word of truth." James 1:18. We can no more live righteous lives by our own strength than we could beget ourselves. The work that is begun by the Spirit must be carried to completion by the Spirit. "We are made partakers of Christ, if we hold the beginning of our confidence steadfast unto the end." Hebrews 3:14, KJV. "He who began a good work in you will bring it to completion at the day of Jesus Christ." Philippians 1:6. And He alone can do it.

⁴ Did you experience so many things in vain?—if it really is in vain. ⁵ Does He who supplies the Spirit to you and works miracles among you do so by works of the law, or by hearing of faith?

These questions show that the experience of the Galatian brethren had been as deep and genuine as would be expected from those before whose eyes Christ was openly crucified. The Spirit had been given to them, miracles had been wrought among them and even by them, for the gifts of the Spirit accompany the gift of the Spirit. And as the result of this living gospel among them they had suffered persecution; for "all that will live godly in Christ Jesus shall suffer persecution." 2 Timothy 3:12, KJV. This makes the case the more serious. Having shared the sufferings of Christ they were now departing from Him. And this departure from Christ, through whom alone righteousness can come, was marked by disobedience to the law of truth. They were insensibly but inevitably transgressing the law to which they were looking for salvation.

⁶ Thus Abraham "believed God, and it was reckoned to him as righteousness."

The questions asked in verses 3, 4 and 5 suggest their own answer. The Spirit was ministered, and miracles were wrought, not by works of law, but by "hearing of faith," that is, by the obedience of faith, for faith comes by hearing the Word of God. Romans 10:17. Thus Paul's labor, and the first experience of the Galatians, were exactly in line with the experience of Abraham, whose faith was accounted for righteousness. Let it be remembered that the "false brethren" who preached "another gospel," even the false gospel of righteousness by works, were Jews and claimed Abraham for their father. It would be their boast that they were "children" of Abraham, and they would appeal to their circumcision as proof of the fact. But the very thing upon which they relied as proving them to be children of Abraham was proof that they were not; for "Abraham 'believed God, and it was reckoned to him as righteousness.'" Abraham had the righteousness of faith before he was circumcised. Romans 4:11. "So you see that it is men of faith who are the sons of Abraham." Galatians 3:7. Abraham was not justified by works (Romans 4:2, 3), but his faith wrought righteousness.

The same trouble still exists. People take the sign for the substance, the end for the means. They see that righteousness reveals itself in good works. Therefore they assume that the good works bring the righteousness. Righteousness gained by faith, good works wrought without working, seem to them impractical and fanciful. They call themselves "practical" men and believe that the only way to have a thing done is to do it. But the truth is that all such men are highly *im*practical. A man absolutely "without strength" cannot do anything, not even so much as to raise himself up to take the medicine that is offered him. Any counsel for him to try to do it would be impractical. Only in the Lord is there righteousness and strength. Isaiah 45:24. "Commit thy way unto the Lord; trust also in Him; and *He* shall bring it to pass. And *He* shall bring forth thy righteousness as the light." Psalm 37:5, 6, KJV. Abraham is the father of all who believe for righteousness, and of those only. The only "practical" thing is to believe, even as he did.

⁷ So you see that it is men of faith who are the sons of Abraham. ⁸ And the scripture, foreseeing that God would justify the Gentiles by faith, preached the gospel beforehand to Abraham, saying, "In you shall all the nations be blessed."

These verses will bear much reading. An understanding of them will guard one against many errors. And it is not difficult to understand; simply hold to what it says, and you have it.

(a) The verse shows us that the gospel was preached at least as early as the days of Abraham.

(b) It was God Himself who preached it. Therefore, it was the true and only gospel.

(c) It was the same gospel that Paul preached. Therefore we have no other gospel than that which Abraham had.

(d) The gospel differs in no particular now from what it was in Abraham's day.

God requires just the same things now that He required then and nothing more.

Moreover, the gospel was then preached to the Gentiles, for Abraham was a "Gentile," or in other words, a heathen. He was brought up as a heathen, for "Terah, the father of Abraham," "served other gods" (Joshua 24:2), and was a heathen until the gospel was preached to him. So the preaching of the gospel to the Gentiles was no new thing in the days of Peter and Paul. The Jewish nation was taken out from among the heathen, and it is only by the preaching of the gospel to the heathen that Israel is built up and saved. See Acts 15:14-18; Romans 11:25, 26. The very existence of the people Israel always was and still is a standing proof that God's purpose is to save people from among the Gentiles. It is in fulfillment of this purpose that Israel exists.

Thus we see that the apostle takes the Galatians (and us), back to the fountainhead, to the place where God Himself preaches the gospel to us "Gentiles." No Gentile can hope to be saved in any other way or by any other gospel than that by which Abraham was saved.

9 So then, those who are men of faith are blessed with Abraham who had faith. **10** For all who rely on works of the law are under a curse; for it is written, "Cursed be every one who does not abide by all things written in the book of the law, and do them."

Mark the close connection between these and the preceding verse. The gospel was preached to Abraham in the words, "In you shall all the nations be blessed." The words "heathen" or "Gentiles," as in the *Revised Standard Version*, and "nations," in verse 8, come from the very same Greek word. This blessing is the advantage of righteousness through Christ, as we learn from Acts 3:25, 26, KJV; "Ye are the children of the prophets, and of the covenant which God made with our fathers, saying unto Abraham, And in thy seed shall all the kindreds of the earth be blessed. Unto you first God, having raised up His Son Jesus, sent Him to bless you, *in turning away every one of you from his iniquities*." Because God preached the gospel to Abraham, saying, "In you shall all the nations be blessed," those who believe are blessed with faithful Abraham. There is no blessing for any man except the blessing Abraham received! And the gospel preached to him is the only gospel for any people under heaven. The name of Jesus, in whom Abraham believed, saves. "There is no other name under heaven given among men by which we must be saved." Acts 4:12. In Him "we have redemption through His blood, even the forgiveness of sins." Colossians 1:14, KJV. The forgiveness of sins carries with it all blessings.

A Contrast: Under the Curse

Note the sharp contrast in verses 9 and 10. "Those who are men of faith are blessed," but "all who rely on works of the law are under a curse." Faith brings the blessing. Works bring the curse, or, rather, leave one under the curse. The curse is on all, for "he who does not believe is condemned already, because he has not believed in the name of the only Son of God." John 3:18. Faith removes the curse.

Who are under the curse? "All who rely on works of the law." Note that it does not say that those who *do* the law are under the curse, for that would be a contradiction of Revelation 22:14, KJV: "*Blessed* are they that *do* His commandments that they may have right to the tree of life, and may enter in through the gates into the city." "*Blessed* are those whose way is blameless, who *walk* in the law of the Lord!" Psalm 119:1.

So, then, they who are of *faith* are keepers of the law; for they who are of faith are blessed, and those who do the commandments are blessed. By faith they do the commandments. Since the gospel is contrary to human nature, we become doers of the law not by doing but by believing. If we *worked* for righteousness, we would be exercising only our own sinful human nature, and so would get no nearer to righteousness, but farther from it. But by *believing* the "exceeding great and precious promises," we become "partakers of the divine nature" (2 Peter 1:4, KJV), and then all our works are wrought in God. "The Gentiles, which followed not after righteousness, have attained to righteousness, even the righteousness which is of faith. But Israel, which followed after the law of righteousness, hath not attained to the law of righteousness. Wherefore? Because they sought it not by faith, but as it were by the works of the law. For they stumbled at that stumbling stone; as it is written, Behold, I lay in Sion a stumbling stone and rock of offense: and whosoever believeth on Him shall not be ashamed." Romans 9:30-33, KJV.

What the Curse Is

No one can read Galatians 3:10 carefully and thoughtfully without seeing that the curse is transgression of the law. Disobedience to God's law is itself the curse; for "sin came into the world through one man and death through sin." Romans 5:12. Sin has death wrapped up in it. Without sin death would be impossible, for "the sting of death is sin." 1 Corinthians 15:56. "For all who rely on works of the law are under a curse." Why? Because the law is a curse? Not by any means: "The law is holy, and the commandment is holy and just and good." Romans 7:12. Why, then, are all who rely on works of the law under a curse? Because it is written, "Cursed be everyone who does not abide by all things written in the book of the law, and do them."

Mark it well: They are not cursed because they *do* the law, but because they do *not* do it. So, then, we see that relying on works of the law does not mean that one is doing the law. No! "The carnal mind is enmity against God: for it is not subject to the law of God, neither indeed *can* be." Romans 8:7, KJV. *All* are under the curse, and he who thinks to get out by his own works, remains there. Since the "curse" consists in not continuing in all things that are written in the law, therefore the "blessing" means perfect conformity to the law.

Blessing and Cursing

"Behold, I set before you this day a blessing and a curse; a blessing, if ye *obey* the commandments of the Lord your God, which I command you this day: and a *curse*, if ye will *not obey* the commandments of the Lord your God." Deuteronomy 11:26-28, KJV. This is the living word of God, addressed to each one of us personally. "The law brings wrath" (Romans 4:15), but the wrath of God comes only on the children of *dis*obedience (Ephesians 5:6). If we truly believe, we are not condemned, because faith brings us into harmony with the law, the life of God. "Whoso looketh into the perfect law of liberty, and continueth therein, he being not a forgetful hearer, but a doer of the work, this man shall be blessed in his deed." James 1:25, KJV.

Good Works

The Bible does not disparage good works. On the contrary, it exalts them. "This is a faithful saying, and these things I will that thou affirm constantly, that they which have believed in God might be careful to maintain good works. These things are good and profitable." Titus 3:8, KJV. The charge against the unbelieving is that they are "unto every good work *reprobate*." Titus 1:16, KJV. Timothy was exhorted to "charge them that are rich in this world," "that they do *good*, that they be rich in good *works*." 1 Timothy 6:17, 18, KJV. And the apostle Paul prayed for us all that we might "walk worthy of the Lord unto all pleasing, being fruitful in *every* good work." Colossians 1:10, KJV. Still further, we are assured that God has created us "in Christ Jesus for good works," "that we should walk in them." Ephesians 2:10.

He has Himself prepared these works for us, wrought them out, and laid them up for all who trust in Him. Psalm 31:19. "This is the work of God, that you believe in Him whom He has sent." John 6:29. Good works are commended, but we cannot do them. They can be performed only by the One who is good, and that is God. If there be ever any good in us, it is God who works in us. There is no disparagement of anything that He does. "Now the God of peace, that brought again from the dead our

Lord Jesus, that great Shepherd of the sheep, through the blood of the everlasting covenant, make you perfect in every good work to do His will, working in you that which is wellpleasing in His sight, through Jesus Christ; to whom be glory forever and ever. Amen." Hebrews 13:20, 21, KJV.

¹¹ Now it is evident that no man is justified before God by the law; for "He who through faith is righteous shall live"; ¹² but the law does not rest on faith, for "He who does them shall live by them."

Who Are the Righteous?

When we read the frequent statement, "He who through faith is righteous shall live," it is necessary to have a clear idea of what the word "righteous" means. The King James Version has it, "The just shall live by faith." To be justified by faith is to be made righteous by faith. "All unrighteousness is sin" (1 John 5:17, KJV), and "sin is the transgression of the law" (1 John 3:4, KJV). Therefore all unrighteousness is transgression of the law, and of course all righteousness is obedience to the law. So we see that the just, or righteous, man is the man who *obeys* the law, and to be justified is to be made a *keeper* of the law.

How to Become Just

Right doing is the end to be obtained, and the law of God is the standard. "The law worketh wrath," because "all have sinned," and "the wrath of God cometh on the children of *dis*obedience." How shall we become doers of the law and thus escape wrath, or the curse? The answer is, "He who through *faith* is righteous shall live." By faith, not by works, we become doers of the law! "With the heart man believeth *unto righteousness*." Romans 10:10, KJV. That no man is justified by the law in the sight of God is evident. How? From this, that "the just shall live by faith." If righteousness came by works, then it would not be by faith; "if it is by grace, it is no longer on the basis of works; otherwise grace would no longer be grace." Romans 11:6. "To him that worketh is the reward not reckoned of grace, but of debt. But to him that worketh not, but believeth on Him that justifieth the ungodly, his faith is counted for righteousness." Romans 4:4, 5, KJV.

There is no exception, no halfway working. It is not said that *some* of the just shall live by faith, or that they shall live by faith *and* works; but simply, "the just shall live by faith." And that proves righteousness comes not by their own works. All of the just are *made* just and *kept* just by faith alone. This is because the law is so holy. It is greater than can be done by man; only divine power can accomplish it; so by faith we receive the Lord Jesus, and He lives the perfect law in us.

The Law Not of Faith

"The law does not rest on faith." Of course it is the written law, no matter whether in a book or on tables of stone, that is here referred to. That law simply says, "Do this," or, "do not do that." "He who does them shall live by them." That is the sole condition on which the written law offers life. Works, and works only, commend themselves to it. How those works are obtained is of no consequence to it, provided they are present. But none have done the requirements of the law, and so there can be no *doers* of the law; that is, none who in their own lives can present a record of perfect obedience.

"He who *does* them shall live by them." But one must be *alive* in order to do! A dead man can do nothing, and he who is "dead in trespasses and sins" can do no righteousness. Christ is the only one in whom there is life, for He is the life, and He alone has done and can do the righteousness of the law. When, instead of being denied and repressed, He is acknowledged and received, He lives in us all the fullness of His life, so that it is no more we but Christ living in us. Then His obedience in us makes us righteous. Our faith is counted for righteousness simply because our faith appropriates the living Christ. In faith we yield our bodies as temples of God. Christ, the Living Stone, is enshrined in the hearts, which become God's thrones. And so in Christ the living law becomes our life, for "out of the heart are the issues of life."

[13] Christ redeemed us from the curse of the law, having become a curse for us—for it is written, "Cursed be every one who hangs on a tree"— [14] that in Christ Jesus the blessing of Abraham might come upon the Gentiles, that we might receive the promise of the Spirit through faith.

The Real Question at Issue

In this letter there is no controversy over the law as to whether or not it should be obeyed. No one had claimed that the law was abolished or changed or had lost its force. The letter contains no hint of any such thing. The question was not *if* the law should be kept but *how* it was to be kept. Justification—being made righteous—was admitted to be a necessity. The question was: "Is it by faith or by works?" The "false brethren" were persuading the Galatians that they must be made righteous by their own efforts. Paul by the Spirit was showing that all such attempts were useless and could result only in fastening the curse more firmly on the sinner.

Righteousness through faith in Jesus Christ is set forth to all men in all time as the only real righteousness. The false teachers made their boast *in the law*, but through breaking it caused the name of God to be blasphemed. Paul made his boast *in Christ*, and by the righteousness of the law to which he thus submitted, he caused the name of God to be glorified in him.

The Sting of Sin

That death is the curse is evident from the last part of verse 13: "Cursed be everyone who hangs on a tree." Christ was made a curse for us in that He hung on a tree, that is, was crucified. But sin is the cause of death: "By one man sin entered into the world, and death by sin; and so death passed upon all men, for that all have sinned." Romans 5:12, KJV. "The sting of death is sin." 1 Corinthians 15:56. So we have the substance of verse 10 thus, that those who do not "abide by all the things written in the law" are *dead*. That is, disobedience is death.

"When lust hath conceived, it bringeth forth sin: and sin, when it is finished, bringeth forth death." James 1:15, KJV. Sin contains death, and men out of Christ are "dead through trespasses and sins." Ephesians 2:1. It matters not that they walk about seemingly full of life. The words of Christ are, "Unless you eat the flesh of the Son of man and drink His blood, you have no life in you." John 6:53. "She that liveth in pleasure is dead while she liveth." 1 Timothy 5:6, KJV. It is a living death—a body of death—that is endured. Romans 7:24. Sin is the transgression of the law. The wages of sin is death. The curse, therefore, is the death that is carried about concealed even in the most attractive sin. "Cursed be everyone who does not abide by all things written in the book of the law, and do them."

Redemption From the Curse

"Christ redeemed us from the curse of the law." Some who superficially read this rush off frantically exclaiming, "We don't need to keep the law, because Christ has redeemed us from the curse of it," as though the text said that Christ redeemed us from the curse of obedience. Such read the Scriptures to no profit. The curse, as we have seen, is *dis*obedience: "Cursed be everyone who does not abide by all things written in the book of the law, and do them." Therefore Christ has redeemed us from *dis*obedience to the law. God sent forth His Son "in the likeness of sinful flesh and for sin, ... in order that the just requirement of the law might be *fulfilled* in us." Romans 8:3, 4.

Someone may lightly say, "Then we are all right; whatever we do is right so far as the law is concerned, since we are redeemed." It is true that all are redeemed, but not all have *accepted* redemption. Many say of Christ, "We will not have this Man to reign over us," and thrust the blessing of God from them. But redemption is for *all*. *All* have been purchased with the precious blood—the life—of Christ, and *all* may be, if they will, free from sin and death. By that blood we are redeemed from "the futile ways inherited from your fathers." 1 Peter 1:18.

Stop and think what this means. Let the full force of the announcement impress itself upon your consciousness. "Christ redeemed us from the curse of the law"—from our failure to continue in all its righteous requirements. We need not sin anymore! He has cut the cords of sin that bound us so that we have but to accept His salvation in order to be free from every besetting sin. It is not necessary for us any longer to spend our lives in earnest longings for a better life and in vain regrets for desires unrealized. Christ raises no false hopes, but He comes to the captives of sin and cries to them, "Liberty! Your prison doors are open. Go forth." What more can be said? Christ has gained the complete victory over this present evil world, over "the lust of the flesh and the lust of the eyes and the pride of life" (1 John 2:16), and our faith in Him makes His victory ours. We have but to accept it.

Christ Made a Curse for Us

That "Christ died for the ungodly" (Romans 5:6) is evident to all who read the Bible. He "was delivered for our offenses." Romans 4:25, KJV. The Innocent suffered for the guilty, the Just for the unjust. "He was wounded for our transgressions. He was bruised for our iniquities: the chastisement of our peace was upon Him; and with His stripes we are healed. All we like sheep have gone astray; we have turned everyone to his own way; and the Lord hath laid on Him the iniquity of us all." Isaiah 53:5, 6, KJV. But death came by sin. Death is the curse that has passed upon all men simply because "all have sinned." So, as Christ was "made a curse for us," it follows that Christ was "made to be sin for us." 2 Corinthians 5:21, KJV. He "bore our sins *in His body*" to the tree. 1 Peter 2:24. Note that our sins were "in His body." It was no superficial work that He undertook. Our sins were not merely figuratively laid on Him, but were "in His body." He was "made a curse" for us, "made to be sin" for us, and consequently suffered death for us.

To some this truth seems repugnant. To the Greeks it is foolishness, to the Jews a stumbling block. But to us who are saved, it is "the power of God." See 1 Corinthians 1:23, 24. Remember that He bore *our sins* in His own body—not His sins, for He never sinned. The same Scripture that tells us He was made to be sin for us, assures us that He "knew no sin." The same text that tells us that He carried our sins "in His own body," is careful to let us know that He "did no sin." The fact that He could carry our sin about with Him and in Him, being actually made to be sin for us, and yet not do any sin, is to His everlasting glory and our eternal salvation from sin. All the sins of all men were on Him, yet no person ever discovered a trace of sin upon Him. No sin was ever manifested in His life, although He took all sin upon Himself. He received it and *swallowed it up* by the *power* of the endless life in which He swallows up death. He can bear sin and yet be untainted by it. It is by this marvelous life that He redeems us. He gives us His life so that we may be freed from every taint of the sin that is in our flesh.

Christ, "in the days of His flesh, when He had offered up prayers and supplications with strong crying and tears unto Him that was able to save Him from death, and was heard in that He feared." Hebrews 5:7, KJV. But He died! No one took His life from Him. He laid it down that He might take it again. John 10:17, 18. The cords of death were loosed, "because it was not possible for Him to be held by it." Acts 2:24. Why was it not possible for death to hold Him, even though He voluntarily put Himself in its power? Because He "knew no sin." He took sin upon Himself but was saved from its power. He was "in all things" "made like unto His brethren," "in all points tempted like as we are" (Hebrews 2:17; 4:15, KJV), and since He could of Himself do nothing (John 5:30), He prayed to the Father to keep Him from being overcome and thereby falling under the power of death. And He was heard. In His case these words were fulfilled: "The Lord God will help Me; therefore shall I not be confounded: therefore have I set My face like a flint, and I know that I shall not be ashamed. He is near that justifieth Me; who will contend with Me?" Isaiah 50:7, 8, KJV.

Whose sin was it that thus oppressed Him, and from which He was delivered? Not His own, for He had none. It was your sin and mine. Our sins have already been overcome—vanquished. We have to fight only with an already defeated foe. When you come to God in the name of Jesus, having surrendered yourself to His death and life so that you do not bear His name in vain because Christ lives in you, you have only to remember that every sin was on Him, and is still on Him, and that He is the conqueror, and straightway you will say, "Thanks be to God, which giveth us the victory through our Lord Jesus Christ." 1 Corinthians 15:57, KJV. "Now thanks be unto God, which always causeth us to triumph in Christ, and maketh manifest the savor of His knowledge by us in every place." 2 Corinthians 2:14, KJV.

The Revelation of the Cross

The "tree" brings us to the inexhaustible subject presented in Galatians 2:20 and 3:1—the ever-present cross:

(1) The redemption from sin and death is accomplished through the cross, Galatians 3:13.

(2) The gospel is all contained in the cross. For the gospel is "the power of God for salvation to everyone who has faith." Romans 1:16. And "to us who are being saved" the cross of Christ "is the power of God." 1 Corinthians 1:18.

(3) Christ is revealed to fallen men only as the crucified and risen One. There is no other name under heaven given among men, whereby salvation may be obtained. Acts 4:12. Therefore it is all that God sets forth before men, since He does not wish to confuse them. "Christ and Him crucified" is all that Paul wished to know. It is all that any man needs to know. The one thing that men need is salvation. If they get that, they get all things. But salvation is found only in the cross of Christ. Therefore God puts before the eyes of men nothing else; He gives them just

what they need. Jesus Christ is by God set forth openly crucified before the eyes of every man, so that there is no excuse for any to be lost or to continue in sin.

(4) Christ is set forth before men as the crucified Redeemer; and since men need to be saved from the curse, He is set forth as bearing the curse. Wherever there is any curse, there is Christ bearing it. We have already seen that Christ bore and still bears our curse of the earth itself, for He bore the crown of thorns, and the curse pronounced on the earth was, "Thorns and thistles it shall bring forth." Genesis 3:18. So the whole creation, which now groans under the curse, has been redeemed through the cross of Christ. See Romans 8:19-23.

(5) On the cross Christ bore the curse. His being made a curse for us was indicated by His hanging on the cross. The cross is the symbol of not only the curse, but also the deliverance from the curse, since it is the cross of Christ, the Conqueror and Deliverer.

(6) Where is the curse? Ah, where is it not? The blindest can see it if he will but acknowledge the evidence of his own senses. Imperfection is a curse, yes, that *is* the curse. And imperfection is on everything connected with this earth. Man is imperfect, and even the finest plant that grows from the earth is imperfect in some respect. Nothing meets the eye but that it shows the possibility of improvement, even if our untrained eyes cannot see the absolute necessity of it. When God made the earth, everything was "very good," or, as the Hebrew idiom has it, "good exceedingly." God Himself could see no chance, no possibility, of improvement. But now it is different. The gardener spends his thought and labor trying to improve the fruits and flowers under his care. And since the best that the earth produces reveals the curse, what need be said of the gnarled, stunted growths, the withered and blasted buds and leaves and fruits, and the noxious, poisonous weeds? Everywhere "a curse devours the earth." Isaiah 24:6.

(7) Should we therefore be discouraged? No. "For God hath not destined us for wrath, but to obtain salvation through our Lord Jesus Christ." 1 Thessalonians 5:9. Although the curse is visible everywhere, yet things live, and men live. But the curse is death, and no man and no thing in creation can bear death and still live. Death kills. But Christ is the living One; He died, but He is alive forevermore. Revelation 1:18. He alone can bear the

curse—death—and on the basis of His own merits return to life. There is life on the earth and in man, in spite of the curse, because Christ died on the cross. Every blade of grass, every leaf of the forest, every shrub and tree, every flower and fruit, even the bread that we eat, is stamped with the cross of Christ. In our own bodies is the stamp of Christ crucified. Everywhere is the evidence of that cross. The preaching of the cross, the gospel, is the power of God, revealed in all things that He has made. That is "the power at work in us." Ephesians 3:20. A comparison of Romans 1:16-20 with 1 Corinthians 1:17, 18 shows clearly that the evidence of the cross of Christ is seen in all the things that God has made—even in our own bodies.

Courage From Despair

"Innumerable evils have compassed me about; mine iniquities have taken hold upon me, so that I am not able to look up; they are more than the hairs of mine head: therefore my heart faileth me." Psalm 40:12, KJV. But not only may we with confidence cry unto God "out of the depths," but God in His infinite mercy has so ordered it that the very depths themselves are a source of confidence. The fact that although we are in the depths of sin we yet live is proof that God Himself, in the person of Christ on the cross, is present with us to deliver us. So through the Holy Spirit everything, even what is under the curse (for everything is under the curse), preaches the gospel. Our own weakness, instead of being a cause of discouragement, is, if we believe the Lord, a pledge of redemption. "Out of weakness" we are "made strong." "In all these things we are more than conquerors through Him who loved us." Romans 8:37. Truly, God has not left Himself without witness among men. "He who believes in the Son of God has the testimony in himself." 1 John 5:10.

The Blessing From the Curse

Christ bore the curse in order that the blessing might come to us. Death to Him is life to us. If we willingly bear about in our bodies the dying of the Lord Jesus, the life also of Jesus will be manifested in our mortal flesh. 2 Corinthians 4:10. He was made to be sin for us, that we might be made the righteousness of God in Him. 2 Corinthians 5:21. The blessing we receive through the curse He bears is the blessing of deliverance from sin. For as the curse results from the transgression of the law (Galatians 3:10), the blessing consists in being turned away from our iniquities (Acts 3:26). Christ suffered the curse, even sin and death, "that the blessing of Abraham might come on the Gentiles through Jesus Christ."

The blessing of Abraham is, as Paul points out in another letter, righteousness by faith: "David also describeth the blessedness of the man, unto whom God imputeth righteousness without works, saying, Blessed are they whose iniquities are forgiven, and whose sins are covered. Blessed is the man to whom the Lord will not impute sin." Romans 4:6-8, KJV.

He shows further that this blessing rests on the Gentiles who believe, as well as on the Jews who believe, because Abraham received it when he was *un*circumcised "to make him the father of *all* who believe." Verse 11.

The blessing is freedom from sin, even as the curse is the doing of sin. As the curse reveals the cross, so that very curse is by the Lord made to proclaim the blessing. The fact that we physically live, although we are sinners, assures us that deliverance from the sin is ours. "While there's life there's hope," says the adage, because the Life is our hope.

Thank God for the blessed hope! The blessing has come upon *all* men. For "as by the offense of one judgment came upon all men to condemnation; even so by the righteousness of One the free gift came upon all men unto justification of life." Romans 5:18, KJV. God, who is no respecter of persons, "has blessed us in Christ with every spiritual blessing in the heavenly places." Ephesians 1:3. The gift is ours to keep. *If anyone has not this blessing, it is because he has not recognized the gift, or has deliberately thrown it away.*

A Finished Work

"Christ redeemed us from the curse of the law," from sin and death. This He did by "being made a curse for us," and so we are freed from all necessity of sinning. Sin can have no dominion over us if we accept Christ in truth and without reserve. This was just as much a present truth in the days of Abraham, Moses, David, and Isaiah, as it is today. More than seven hundred years before the cross was raised on Calvary, Isaiah, who testified of the things which he understood because his own sin had been purged by a "live coal" from God's alter, said: "Surely He hath borne our griefs, and carried our sorrows. ... He was wounded for our transgressions, He was bruised for our iniquities; the chastisement of our peace was upon Him; and with His stripes we are healed. ... The Lord hath laid on Him the iniquity of us all." Isaiah 53:4-6, KJV. "I have blotted out, as a thick cloud, thy transgressions, and, as a cloud, thy sins: return unto Me; for I have redeemed thee." Isaiah 44:22, KJV. Long before Isaiah's time, David wrote: "He hath not dealt with us after our sins; nor rewarded us according to our iniquities." "As far as the east is from the west, so far hath He removed our transgressions from us." Psalm 103:10, 12, KJV.

"We who have believed enter that rest," because the "works were finished from the foundation of the world." Hebrews 4:3. The blessing that we received is "the blessing of Abraham." We have no other foundation than that of the apostles and prophets, with Christ Himself as the Chief Cornerstone. Ephesians 2:20. It is a full and complete salvation that God has provided. It awaits us as we come into the world. And we do not relieve God of any burden by rejecting it, nor do we add to His labor by accepting it.

"The Promise of the Spirit"

Christ has redeemed us "that we might receive the promise of the Spirit through faith." Do not make the mistake of reading this as though it were "that we might receive the promise of the gift of the Spirit." It does not say that, and it does not mean that, as a little thought will show. Christ *has* redeemed us, and that fact proves the gift of the Spirit, for it was only "through the eternal Spirit" that He offered Himself without spot to God. Hebrews 9:14. But for the Spirit, we should not know that we were sinners. Much less should we know redemption. The Spirit convinces of sin and of righteousness. John 16:8. "It is the Spirit that beareth witness, because the Spirit is truth." 1 John 5:6, KJV. "He that believeth ... hath the witness in himself." Verse 10, KJV. Christ is crucified for every man. That, as we have already seen, is shown in the fact that we are all under the curse, and Christ alone on the cross bears the curse. But it is through the Spirit that Christ dwells on earth among men. Faith enables us to receive the testimony of this witness and rejoice in that which the possession of the Spirit assures.

Note further: The blessing of Abraham comes on us in order that we may receive the promise of the Spirit. But it is only through the Spirit that the blessing comes. Therefore the blessing cannot bring to us the promise that we shall receive the Spirit. We already have the Spirit *with* the blessing. But, having the blessing of the Spirit (namely, righteousness), we are sure of receiving that which the Spirit promises to the righteous, namely, an everlasting inheritance. In blessing Abraham, God promised him an inheritance. The Spirit is the pledge of *all* good.

The Spirit, the Pledge of Inheritance

All God's gifts are in themselves promises of more. There is always much more to follow. God's purpose in the gospel is to gather together in one all things in Jesus Christ, "in whom also we have obtained an inheritance, ... in whom also after that [or when] ye believed, ye were sealed with that Holy Spirit of promise, *which is the earnest of our inheritance* until the redemption of the purchased possession, unto the praise of His glory." Ephesians 1:11-14, KJV.

Of this inheritance we must speak further later on. Suffice it now to say that it is the inheritance promised to Abraham, whose children we become by faith. The inheritance belongs to *all* who are children of God through faith in Christ Jesus. And the Spirit that marks our sonship is the promise, the pledge, the firstfruits of that inheritance. Those who accept Christ's glorious deliverance from the curse of the law—redemption not from obedience to the law, for obedience is not a curse, but from *dis*obedience to the law—have in the Spirit a taste of the power and the blessing of the world to come.

[15] To give a human example, brethren: no one annuls even a man's will, or adds to it, once it has been ratified. [16] Now the promises were made to Abraham and to his offspring. It does not say, "And to offsprings," referring to many; but, referring to one, "And to your offspring," which is Christ. [17] This is what I mean: the law, which came four hundred and thirty years afterward, does not annul a covenant previously ratified by God, so as to make the promise void. [18] For if the inheritance is by the law, it is no longer by promise; but God gave it to Abraham by a promise.

The gospel of worldwide salvation was preached to Abraham.

He believed and received the blessing of righteousness. *All* who believe are blessed with Abraham who believed. Those who are "of faith" are the children of Abraham. "The promises were made to Abraham and to his offspring." "If the inheritance is by the law, it is no longer by promise; but God gave it to Abraham by a promise." The promise made to us is the same promise made to Abraham, the promise of an inheritance in which we share as his children.

"And to His Offspring"

Here is no play upon words. The issue is vital. The controversy is over the *way* of salvation, whether by Christ alone, or by something else, or by Christ *and* something or somebody else. Many people imagine that *they* must save themselves by making themselves good. Many others think that Christ is a valuable adjunct, a good Assistant to their efforts. Others are willing to give Him the *first* place, but not the *only* place. They regard themselves as good seconds. It is the Lord *and* they who do the work. But our text shuts off all such assumption and self-assertion. Not "offsprings," but *the* "*offspring.*" Not many, but *one.* "'And to your offspring,' which is Christ." Christ is the One.

Not Two Lines

We can contrast the "spiritual offspring" with the "fleshly offspring" of Abraham. The opposite of the *spiritual* is *fleshly*, and the fleshly children, unless they are also spiritual children, have no share whatever in the spiritual inheritance. It is possible for men walking about in the body in this world to be wholly spiritual. And such they must be or else they are not children of Abraham. "Those who are in the flesh cannot please God." Romans 8:8. "Flesh and blood cannot inherit the kingdom of God." 1 Corinthians 15:50. There is only one line of spiritual descendants from Abraham, only one set of real spiritual children, and they are those who are "of faith"—those who, by receiving Christ by faith, receive power to become sons of God.

Many Promises in One

But while the "offspring" is singular, the promises are plural. God has nothing for any man that was not promised to Abraham. All the promises of God are conveyed in Christ, in whom Abraham believed. "For all the promises of God find their Yes in Him.

That is why we utter the Amen through Him, to the glory of God." 2 Corinthians 1:20.

The Promised Inheritance

That the thing promised, and the sum of all the promises, is an inheritance is clearly seen from Galatians 3:15-18. The sixteenth verse tells us that the law, coming in four hundred and thirty years after the promise was made and confirmed, cannot make that promise of none effect. "For if the inheritance is by the law, it is no longer by promise; but God gave it to Abraham by a promise." Verse 18. What this promised inheritance is may be seen by comparing the verse just quoted with Romans 4:13: "The promise to Abraham and his descendants, that they should inherit the world, did not come through the law but through the righteousness of faith." And so, although the heavens and earth which are now "reserved unto fire against the day of judgment and perdition of ungodly men," when "the heavens being on fire shall be dissolved, and the elements shall melt with fervent heat," "we, according to His promise, look for new heavens and a new earth, wherein dwelleth righteousness." 2 Peter 3:7, 12, 13, KJV. This is the heavenly country for which Abraham, Isaac, and Jacob looked.

An Inheritance Without Curse

"Christ redeemed us from the curse ... that we might receive the promise of the Spirit through faith." This "promise of the Spirit" we have seen to be the possession of the whole earth made new—redeemed from the curse. For "the creation itself will be set free from its bondage to decay and obtain the glorious liberty of the children of God." Romans 8:21. The earth fresh and new from the hand of God, perfect in every respect, was given to man for a possession. Genesis 1:27, 28, 31. Man sinned and brought the curse upon himself. Christ has taken the whole curse, both of man and of all creation, upon Himself. He redeems the earth from the curse, that it may be the everlasting possession that God originally designed it to be; and He also redeems man from the curse, that he may be fitted for the possession of such an inheritance. This is the sum of the gospel. "The free gift of God is eternal life in Jesus Christ our Lord." Romans 6:23. This gift of eternal life is included in the promise of the inheritance, for God promised the land to Abraham and to his seed for "an everlasting possession." Genesis 17:8. It is an inheritance of righteousness, because the promise that Abraham should be heir of the world was through the righteousness of faith. Righteousness, eternal life, and a place in which to live eternally—these are all in the promise, and they are all that could possibly be desired or given. To redeem man, but to give him no place in which to live, would be an incomplete work. The two actions are parts of one whole. The power by which we are redeemed is the power of creation, by which the heavens and the earth are made new. When all is accomplished, "there shall be no more curse." Revelation 22:3, KJV.

The Covenants of Promise

The covenant and promise of God are one and the same. This is clearly seen from Galatians 3:17, where Paul asserts that to disannul the covenant would be to make void the promise. In Genesis 17 we read that God made a *covenant* with Abraham to give him the land of Canaan for an everlasting possession. Galatians 3:18 says that God gave it to him by *promise*. God's covenants with men can be nothing else than promises to them: "Who hath first given to Him, and it shall be recompensed unto him again? For of Him, and through Him, and to Him, are all things." Romans 11:35, 36, KJV.

After the Flood God made a "covenant" with every beast of the earth, and with every fowl; but the beasts and the birds did not promise anything in return. Genesis 9:9-16. They simply received the favor at the hand of God. That is all we can do—receive. God promises us everything that we need, and more than we can ask, or think, as a gift. We give Him ourselves, that is, nothing. And He gives us Himself, that is, everything. That which makes all the trouble is that even when men are willing to recognize the Lord at all they want to make bargains with Him. They want it to be an equal, "mutual" affair—a transaction in which they can consider themselves on a par with God. But whoever deals with God must deal with Him on His own terms, that is, on a basis of fact—that we have nothing and are nothing, and He has everything and is everything and gives everything.

The Covenant Ratified

The covenant (that is, the promise of God to give men the whole earth made new after having made them free from the

71

curse) was "previously ratified by God." Christ is the Surety of the new covenant, even the everlasting covenant. "For all the promises of God find their Yes in Him. That is why we utter the Amen through Him, to the glory of God." 2 Corinthians 1:20. In Him we have obtained the inheritance (1 Peter 1:3, 4), for the Holy Spirit is the firstfruits of the inheritance, and the possession of the Holy Spirit is Christ Himself dwelling in the heart by faith. God blessed Abraham, saying, "In thy seed shall all the kindreds of the earth be blessed," and this is fulfilled in Christ, whom God has sent to bless us in *turning us away* from our iniquities. Acts 3:25, 26, KJV.

It was the oath of God that ratified the covenant made to Abraham. That promise and that oath to Abraham become our ground of hope, our strong consolation. They are "sure and steadfast" (Hebrews 6:19), because the oath sets forth Christ as the pledge, the surety, and "He always lives" (Hebrews 9:25). He upholds all things by His word of power. Hebrews 1:3. "In Him all things hold together." Colossians 1:17. Therefore "when God desired to show more convincingly to the heirs of the promise the unchangeable character of His purpose, He interposed with an oath." Hebrews 6:17. This is our consolation and hope in fleeing for refuge from sin. He pledged His own existence, and with it the entire universe, for our salvation. Surely a firm foundation for our hope is laid in His excellent Word!

The Law Cannot Make the Promise Void

Do not forget as we proceed that the covenant and the promise are the same thing, and that it conveys land, even the whole earth made new, to Abraham and his children. Remember also that since only righteousness will dwell in the new heavens and the new earth, the promise includes the making righteous of all who believe. This is done in Christ, in whom the promise is confirmed. Now, "no one annuls even a man's will, or adds to it, once it has been ratified." How much more must this be the case with God's "will"!

Therefore, since perfect and everlasting righteousness was assured by the "will" made with Abraham, which was also confirmed in Christ, by the oath of God, it is impossible that the law which was spoken four hundred and thirty years later could introduce any new feature. The inheritance was given to Abraham by *promise*. But if after four hundred and thirty years it should develop that now the inheritance must be gained in some other way, then the promise would be of no effect, and the "will" or covenant would be made void. But *that* would involve the overthrow of God's government and the ending of His existence. For He pledged His own existence to *give* Abraham and his seed the inheritance and the righteousness necessary for it. "For the promise, that he should be the heir of the world, was not to Abraham, or to his seed, through the law, but through the righteousness of faith." Romans 4:13, KJV. The gospel was as full and complete in the days of Abraham as it has ever been or ever will be. No addition to it or change in its provisions or conditions could possibly be made after God's oath to Abraham. Nothing can be taken away from it as it thus existed, and not one thing can ever be required from any man more than what was required of Abraham.

¹⁹ Why then the law? It was added because of transgressions, till the offspring should come to whom the promise had been made; and it was ordained by angels through an intermediary. ²⁰ Now an intermediary implies more than one; but God is one.

"Why then the law?" The apostle Paul asks this question that he may the more emphatically show the place of the law in the gospel. The question is a very natural one. Since the inheritance is wholly by promise, and a "will" or covenant confirmed cannot be changed (nothing can be taken from it, and nothing added to it), why did the law come in four hundred and thirty years afterward? "Why then the law?" What business has it here? What part does it act? Of what use is it?

"It was added because of transgressions." Let it be understood that "the entering of the law" at Sinai was not the beginning of its existence. The law of God existed in the days of Abraham and was kept by him. Genesis 26:5. The law of God existed before it was spoken upon Sinai. Exodus 16:1-4, 27, 28. It was "added" in the sense that at Sinai it was given in more explicit detail.

"Because of transgressions," "Moreover the law entered, that the offense might abound" (Romans 5:20, KJV), in other words, "that sin by the commandment might become exceeding sinful" (Romans 7:13, KJV). It was given under circumstances of the most awful majesty as a warning to the children of Israel that by their unbelief they were in danger of losing the promised inheritance. They did not, like Abraham, believe the Lord; and "whatever does not proceed from faith is sin." Romans 14:23. But the inheritance was promised "through the righteousness of *faith*." Romans 4:13. Therefore the unbelieving Jews could not receive it.

So the law was spoken to them to convince them that they had not the righteousness necessary for the possession of the inheritance. For, although righteousness does not *come* by the law, it must be "witnessed by the law." Romans 3:21, KJV. In short, the law was given to show them that they had not faith and so were not true children of Abraham, and were therefore in a fair way to lose the inheritance. God would have put His law into their hearts even as He put it into Abraham's heart, if they had believed. But when they disbelieved, yet still professed to be heirs of the promise, it was necessary to show them in the most marked manner that their unbelief was sin. The law was spoken because of transgression, or (what is the same thing) because of the unbelief of the people.

Self-confidence Is Sin

The people of Israel were full of self-confidence and of unbelief in God, as is shown by their murmuring against God's leading and by their assumption of the ability to do anything that God required, to fulfill His promises. Exodus 19:8. They had the same spirit as their descendants, who asked, "What must we *do*, to be doing the work of God?" John 6:28. They were so ignorant of God's righteousness that they thought that they could establish their own righteousness as an equivalent. Romans 10:3. Unless they saw their sin, they could not avail themselves of the promise. Hence the necessity of the speaking of the law.

The Ministration of Angels

"Are they not all ministering spirits sent forth to serve, for the sake of those who are to obtain salvation?" Hebrews 1:14. Just what office the thousands of angels who were at Sinai had to perform we cannot know. But we do know that angels have a close and deep interest in everything that concerns man. When the foundations of the earth were laid, "all the sons of God shouted for joy." Job 38:7. A multitude of the heavenly host sang praises when the birth of the Saviour of mankind was announced. These beings who "excel in strength" attend the King of kings, waiting to do His pleasure, "harkening unto the voice of His word." Psalm 103:20, KJV. The fact that they were present at the giving of the law shows that it was an event of the greatest magnitude and importance.

"Through an Intermediary"

The law was given to the people from Sinai "through an intermediary" (or "mediator," KJV). Who was this Mediator? There can be only one answer: "There is one God, and there is one Mediator between God and men, the Man Christ Jesus." 1 Timothy 2:5. "Now an intermediary implies more than one; but God is one." God and Christ Jesus are one. Christ Jesus is both God and man. In mediating between God and man, Christ Jesus represents God to man and man to God. "God was in Christ reconciling the world to Himself." 2 Corinthians 5:19. There is and can be no other mediator between God and men. "Neither is there salvation in any other; for there is none other name under heaven given among men, whereby we must be saved." Acts 4:12, KJV.

Christ's Work as Mediator

Man has wandered from God and rebelled against Him. "All we like sheep have gone astray." Isaiah 53:6. Our iniquities have separated between us and Him. Isaiah 59:1, 2. "The carnal mind is enmity against God: for it is not subject to the law of God, neither indeed can be." Romans 8:7, KJV. Christ came that He might destroy the enmity and reconcile us to God; for He is our peace. See Ephesians 2:14-16. Christ "died for our sins once for all, the righteous for the unrighteous, that He might bring us to God." 1 Peter 3:18. Through Him we have access to God. Romans 5:1, 2; Ephesians 2:18. In Him the carnal mind, the rebellious mind, is taken away, and the mind of the Spirit is given in its stead, "in order that the just requirements of the law might be fulfilled in us, who walk not according to the flesh but according to the Spirit." Romans 8:4. Christ's work is to save that which was lost, to restore that which was broken, to reunite that which was separated. His name is "God with us." With Him dwelling in us we are made "partakers of the divine nature." 2 Peter 1:4.

Christ's work as "intermediary" is not limited in either time or extent. To be mediator means more than to be intercessor. Christ was mediator before sin came into the world, and will be mediator when no sin is in the universe, and no need remains for forgiveness. "In Him all things hold together." He is the very impress of the Father's being. He is the life. Only in and through Him does the life of God flow to all creation. He is then the means, medium, mediator, the way, by which the light of life pervades the universe. He did not first become mediator at the fall of man, but was such from eternity. *No one, not simply no man, but no created being, comes to the Father but by Christ.* No angel can stand in the divine presence except in Christ. No new power was developed, no new machinery, so to speak, was required to be set in motion by the entering of sin into the world. The power that had created all things only continued in God's infinite mercy to work for the restoration of that which was lost. In Christ were all things created; and, therefore, in Him we have redemption through His blood. See Colossians 1:14-17. The power that pervades and upholds the universe is the same power that saves us. "Now unto Him that is able to do exceeding abundantly above all that we ask or think, according to the power that worketh in us, unto Him be glory in the church by Christ Jesus throughout all ages, world without end. Amen." Ephesians 3:20, KJV.

²¹ Is the law then against the promises of God? Certainly not; for if a law had been given which could make alive, then righteousness would indeed be by the law. ²² But the Scripture consigned all things to sin, that the promise by faith of Jesus Christ might be given to those who believe.

"Is the law then against the promises of God?" Not at all. If it were, it would not be in the hands of the Mediator, Christ, for all the promises of God are in Him. 2 Corinthians 1:20. We find the law and the promise combined in Christ. We may know that the law was not and is not against the promises of God from the fact that God gave *both* the promise and the law. We know also that the giving of the law introduced no new element into the "covenant," since, having been confirmed, nothing could be added to or taken from it. But the law is not useless, else God would not have given it. It is not a matter of indifference whether we keep it or not, for God commands it. But all the same it is not against the promise and brings no new element in. Why? Simply because *the law is in the promise.* The promise of the Spirit includes: "I will put My laws into their minds, and write them on their hearts." Hebrews 8:10. And this is what God had done for Abraham when He gave him the covenant of circumcision. Read Romans 4:11; 2:25-29; Philippians 3:3.

The Law Magnifies the Promise

The law is righteousness, as God says: "Hearken to Me, you who know righteousness, the people in whose heart is My law." Isaiah 51:7. So, then, the righteousness which the law demands is the only righteousness that can inherit the promised land. It is obtained, not by the works of the law, but by faith. The righteousness of the law is not attained by human efforts to do the law, but by faith. See Romans 9:30-32. Therefore, the greater the righteousness which the law demands, the greater is seen to be the promise of God. For He has promised to give it to all who believe. Yes, He has sworn it. When, therefore, the law was spoken from Sinai "out of the midst of the fire, of the cloud, and of the thick darkness, with a great voice" (Deuteronomy 5:22, KJV), accompanied by the sounding of the trump of God and with the whole earth quaking at the presence of the Lord and His holy angels, the inconceivable greatness and majesty of the law of God was shown. To everyone who remembered the oath of God to Abraham it was a revelation of the wondrous greatness of God's promise; for all the righteousness which the law demands He has sworn to give to everyone who trusts Him. The "loud voice" with which the law was spoken was the loud voice that from the mountaintops proclaims the glad tidings of the saving mercy of God. See Isaiah 40:9. God's precepts are promises; they *must* necessarily be such, because He knows that we have no power! All that God requires is what He *gives*. When He says, "Thou shalt not," we may take it as His assurance that if we but believe Him He will preserve us from the sin against which He warns us.

Righteousness and Life

"If a law had been given which could make alive, then righteousness would indeed be by the law." This shows us that righteousness is life. It is no mere formula, no dead theory or dogma, but is living action. Christ is the life, and He is, therefore, our righteousness. The law written on two tables of stone could not give life any more than could the stones on which it was written. All its precepts are perfect, but the flinty characters cannot transform themselves into action. He who receives only the law in letter has a "ministration of condemnation" and death. But "the Word was made *flesh.*" In Christ, the Living Stone, the law is life and peace. Receiving *Him* through the "ministration of the Spirit," we have the life of righteousness which the law approves.

This twenty-first verse shows that the giving of the law was to emphasize the importance of the promise. All the circumstances attending the giving of the law—the trumpet, the voice, the earthquake, the fire, the tempest, the thunders and lightnings, the death boundary around the mount—told that "the law worketh wrath" to "the children of *dis*obedience." But the very fact that the wrath which the law works comes only on the children of *dis*obedience proves that the law is good, and that "he who does them shall live by them." Did God wish to discourage the people? Not by any means. The law must be kept, and *the terrors of Sinai were designed to drive them back to the oath of God, which four hundred and thirty years before had been given to stand to all people in all ages as the assurance of righteousness through the crucified and ever-living Saviour.*

How We Learn to Feel Our Need

Jesus said of the Comforter, "When He comes, He will convince the world of sin and of righteousness and of judgment." John 16:8. Of Himself He said, "I came not to call the righteous but *sinners* to repentance." "They that are whole have no need of the physician, but they that are *sick.*" Mark 2:17, KJV. A man must feel his need before he will accept help; he must know his disease before he can apply the remedy.

Even so the promise of righteousness will be utterly unheeded by one who does not realize that he is a sinner. The first part of the "comforting" work of the Holy Spirit therefore is to convince men of sin. So "the Scripture hath concluded all under sin, that the promise by faith of Jesus Christ might be given to them that believe." Galatians 3:22, KJV. "Through the law comes knowledge of sin." Romans 3:20. He who knows that he is a sinner is in the way to acknowledge it; and "if we confess our sins, He is faithful and just, and will forgive our sins and cleanse us from all unrighteousness." 1 John 1:9.

Thus the law is in the hands of the Spirit an active agent in inducing men to accept the fullness of the promise. No one hates the man who has saved his life by pointing out to him an unknown peril. On the contrary, such a one is regarded as a friend and is always remembered with gratitude. Even so will the law be regarded by the one who has been prompted by its warning voice to flee from the wrath to come. He will ever say with the psalmist, "I hate vain thoughts: but Thy law do I love." Psalm 119:113, KJV.

23 Now before faith came, we were confined under the law, kept under restraint until faith should be revealed.

Note the similarity between verses 8 and 22. "The Scripture hath concluded [that is, shut up] all under sin, that the promise by faith of Jesus Christ might be given to them that believe." Verse 22, KJV. "The Scripture, foreseeing that God would justify the Gentiles by faith, preached the gospel beforehand to Abraham, saying, In you shall all the nations be blessed." Verse 8, KJV. We see that the gospel is preached by the same thing (the Scripture) that "consigns" men under sin. The word "conclude" means literally "confine," just as is given in verse 23. Of course, a person who is confined by the law is in prison. In human governments a criminal is confined as soon as the law can get hold of him. God's law is everywhere present and always active. Therefore *the instant a man sins he is confined.* This is the condition of all the world, "for all have sinned," and "there is none righteous, no, not one."

Those disobedient ones to whom Christ preached in the days of Noah were in prison. See 1 Peter 3:19, 20. But they, like all other sinners, were "prisoners of hope." Zechariah 9:12. God "hath looked down from the height of His sanctuary; from heaven did the Lord behold the earth; to hear the groaning of the prisoner; to loose those that are appointed to death." Psalm 102:19, 20, KJV. Christ is given "for a covenant of the people, for a light of the Gentiles; to open the blind eyes, to bring out the prisoners from the prison, and them that sit in darkness out of the prison house." Isaiah 42: 6, 7, KJV.

Let me speak from personal experience to the one who does not yet know the joy and freedom of the Lord. Someday, if not already, you will be sharply convicted of sin by the Spirit of God. You may have been full of doubts and quibbles, of ready answers and self-defense, but then you will have nothing to say. You will then have no doubt about the reality of God and the Holy Spirit and will need no argument to assure you of it; you will know the voice of God speaking to your soul and will feel, as did ancient Israel, "Let not God speak with us, lest we die." Exodus 20:10. Then you will know what it is to be "confined" in a prison whose walls seem to close on you, not only barring all escape, but seeming to suffocate you. The tales of people condemned to be buried alive with a heavy stone upon them will seem very vivid and real to you as you feel the tables of the law crushing out your life, and a hand of marble seems to be breaking your very heart. Then it will give you joy to remember that you are shut up for the sole purpose that "the promise by faith of Jesus Christ" might be accepted by you. As soon as you lay hold of that promise, you will find it to be the key that unlocks any door in your "Doubting Castle" (see *The Pilgrim's Progress*). The prison doors will fly open and you will say, "Our soul is escaped as a bird out of the snare of the fowlers; the snare is broken, and we are escaped." Psalm 124:7, KJV.

Under the Law, Under Sin

Before faith came we were confined under the law, "shut up" unto the faith which should afterward be revealed. We know that whatsoever is not of faith is sin (Romans 14:23); therefore, to be "under the law" is identical with being under sin. The grace of God brings salvation from sin so that when we believe God's grace we are no longer under the law, because we are freed from sin. *Those who are under the law therefore are the transgressors of the law.* The righteous are not under it, but are walking in it.

²⁴ So that the law was our custodian until Christ came, that we might be justified by faith.

The Revised Standard Version renders "custodian" in the place of the King James Version's "schoolmaster." The German and Scandinavian translations employ a word which signifies "master of a house of correction."

The Greek word comes down to us in English as "pedagogue." The *paidagogos* was the father's slave who accompanied the father's boys to school to see that they did not play truant. If they attempted to run away he would bring them back and had authority even to beat them to keep them in the way. The word has come to be used as meaning "schoolmaster," although the Greek word does not convey the idea of a schoolmaster. "Supervisor" or "custodian" would be better. The one under this custodian, although nominally at large, is really deprived of his liberty just the same as though he were actually in a cell. The fact is that all who do not believe are "under sin," "shut up" "under the law," and, therefore, the law acts as their supervisor or custodian. It is the law that will not let them go. The guilty cannot escape in their guilt. Although God is merciful and gracious, He will not clear the guilty. Exodus 34:6, 7. That is, He will not lie by calling evil good. *But He provides a way by which the guilty may lose their guilt.* Then the law will no longer curtail their liberty and they can walk free in Christ.

Freedom in Christ

Christ says, "I am the door," John 10:9. He is also the sheepfold and the Shepherd. Men fancy that when they are outside the fold they are free, and that to come into the fold would mean a curtailing of their liberty; but exactly the reverse is true. The fold of Christ is "a large place," while unbelief makes a narrow prison. The sinner can have but a narrow range of thought. The true free thinker is the one who comprehends "with all saints what is the breadth and length and height and depth," of "the love of Christ, which surpasses knowledge." Ephesians 3:18, 19. Outside of Christ is bondage. In Him alone there is freedom. Outside of Christ, the man is in prison, "caught in the toils of his sin." Proverbs 5:22.

"The power of sin is the law." 1 Corinthians 15:56. It is the law that declares a man to be a sinner and makes him conscious of his condition. "Through the law comes knowledge of sin," and "sin is not counted where there is no law." Romans 3:20; 5:13. The law really forms the sinner's prison walls. They close in on him, making him feel uncomfortable, oppressing him with a sense of sin, as though they would press his life out. While in vain he makes frantic efforts to escape, those commandments stand as firm prison walls. Whichever way he turns he finds a command-ment which says to him, "You can find no freedom by me, for you have sinned." If he seeks to make friends with the law and promises to keep it, he is no better off, for his sin still remains. It goads him and drives him to the only way of escape—"the promise by faith of Jesus Christ." In Christ he is made "free indeed," for in Christ he is made the righteousness of God. In Christ is "the perfect law of liberty."

The Law Preaches the Gospel

All creation speaks of Christ, proclaiming the power of His salvation. Every fiber of man's being cries out for Christ. Men do not realize it, but Christ is "the Desire of all nations." Haggai 2:7, KJV. He alone satisfies "The desire of every living thing." Psalm 145:16. Only in Him can relief be found for the world's unrest and longing.

Now since Christ, in whom is peace ("for He is our peace"), is seeking the weary and heavy-laden and calling them to Himself (Matthew 11:28-30), and since every man has longings that nothing else in the world can satisfy, it is clear that if the man is awakened by the law to keener consciousness of his condition, and the law continues goading him, giving him no rest, shutting up every other way of escape, *the man must at last find the door of safety,* for it stands open. Christ is the city of refuge to which everyone pursued by the avenger of blood may flee, sure of finding a welcome. In Christ alone will the sinner find release from the lash of the law, for in Christ the righteousness of the law is fulfilled, and by Him it is fulfilled in us. Romans 8:4. The law will allow nobody to be saved unless he has "the righteousness which is of God by faith," the faith of Jesus Christ.

²⁵ But now that faith has come, we are no longer under a custodian; ²⁶ for in Christ Jesus you are all sons of God, through faith.

"Faith cometh by hearing, and hearing by the Word of God." Romans 10:17, KJV. Whenever a man receives the word of God, the word of promise, which brings with it the fullness of the law, and no longer fights against it, but yields to it, faith comes to him. The eleventh chapter of Hebrews shows that faith came from the beginning. Since the days of Abel men have found freedom by faith. Faith can come now, today. "Now is the acceptable time; behold, now is the day of salvation." 2 Corinthians 6:2. "Today, when you hear His voice, do not harden your hearts." Hebrews 3:7.

²⁷ For as many of you as were baptized into Christ have put on Christ.

"Do you know that all of us who have been baptized into Christ

Jesus were baptized into His death?" Romans 6:3. It is by His death that Christ redeems us from the curse of the law; *but we must die with Him.* Baptism is "the likeness of His death." We rise to walk "in newness of life," even Christ's life. See Galatians 2:20. Having put on Christ, we are one in Him. We are completely identified with Him. Our identity is lost in His. It is often said of one who has been converted, "He is so changed you would not know him. He is not the same man." No, he is not. God has turned him into another man. Therefore, being one with Christ, he has a right to whatever Christ has, and a right to "the heavenly places" where Christ sits. From the prison house of sin he is exalted to the dwelling place of God. This of course presupposes that baptism is to him a reality, not a mere outward form. It is not simply into the visible *water* that he is baptized, but "into *Christ,*" into His life.

How Baptism Saves Us

The Greek word for "baptize" means to plunge into, to immerse. The Greek blacksmith baptized his iron in the water to cool it. The housewife baptized her dishes in water in order to clean them. And for the same purpose all would "baptize" their hands in water. Yes, every man would "baptize" himself frequently, going to the *baptisterion*, that is, the immersing pool, for that purpose. We have the same word transferred as "baptistery." It was and is a place where people could plunge in and be wholly immersed in water.

Being "baptized into Christ" indicates what must be our relation to Him. We must be swallowed up and lost to sight in His life. Only Christ will henceforth be seen, so that it is no more I, but Christ; for "we were buried ... with Him by baptism into death." Romans 6:4. Baptism saves us "through the resurrection of Jesus Christ" from the dead (1 Peter 3:21), because we are baptized into His death, "so that as Christ was raised from the dead by the glory of the Father, we too might walk in newness of life." Being reconciled to God by the death of Christ, we are "saved by His life." Romans 5:10. So baptism into Christ, not the mere form, but the fact, does save us.

This baptism is "the answer of a good conscience toward God." 1 Peter 3:21, KJV. If there is not a good conscience toward God, there is no Christian baptism. Therefore, the person to be baptized must be old enough to have a conscience in the matter. He must have a consciousness of sin, and also of forgiveness by Christ. He must know the life that is manifested, and must willingly give up his old life of sin for the new life of righteousness.

Baptism is "not the putting away of the filth of the flesh" (1 Peter 3:21, KJV), not the outward cleansing of the body, but the purging of the soul and conscience. There is a fountain opened for sin and for uncleanness (Zechariah 13:1), and in this fountain runs the blood of Christ. Christ's life flows in a stream from the throne of God in the midst of which is the slain Lamb (Revelation 5:6), even as it flowed from the side of Christ on the cross. When "through the eternal Spirit" He had offered Himself to God, there flowed from His side blood and water. John 19:34. Christ "loved the church, and gave Himself for it; that He might sanctify and cleanse it with the washing of water by the word." Ephesians 5:25, 26, KJV. Literally, "a water bath in the Word." In being buried in the water in the name of the Father, the Son, and the Holy Spirit, the conscientious believer signifies his acceptance of the water of life, the blood of Christ, which cleanses from all sin, and that he gives himself to live henceforth by every word that proceeds out of the mouth of God. From that time he disappears from sight, and only the life of Christ is manifested in his mortal flesh.

28 There is neither Jew nor Greek, there is neither slave nor free, there is neither male nor female; for you are all one in Christ Jesus. 29 And if you are Christ's, then you are Abraham's offspring, heirs according to the promise.

"There is no difference." This is a keynote of the gospel. All are alike sinners, and all are saved in the same way. They who would make a distinction on the ground of nationality, claiming that there is something different for the Jew than for the Gentile, might just as well make a difference on the ground of sex, claiming that women cannot be saved in the same way and at the same time as men. There is but one way. All human beings, of whatever race or condition, are equal before God. "You are all one in Christ Jesus," and Christ is the One. "It does not say, 'And to offsprings,' referring to many; but, referring to one, 'and to your offspring,' which is Christ." Galatians 3:16. There is but one "Offspring," but it embraces all who are Christ's.

In putting on Christ, we "put on the new nature, created after the likeness of God in true righteousness and holiness." Ephesians 4:24. He has abolished in His flesh the enmity, the carnal mind, "that He might create in Himself one new man in place of the two." Ephesians 2:15. He alone is the real man, "the Man Christ Jesus." Outside of Him there is no real manhood. We come unto "a perfect man" only when we arrive at "the measure of the stature of the fullness of Christ." Ephesians 4:13. In the fullness of time God will gather together in one all things in Christ. There will be but one Man and only one Man's righteousness, even as the "offspring" is but one. "If you are Christ's, then you are Abraham's offspring, heirs according to the promise."

Christ is the "Offspring." That is plainly stated. But Christ did not live for Himself. He has won an inheritance, not for Himself, but for His brethren. God's purpose is to "gather together in one all things in Christ." Ephesians 1:10, KJV. He will finally put an end to divisions of every kind and He does it now in those who accept Him. In Christ there are no distinctions of nationality, and no classes and ranks. The Christian thinks of any other man—English, German, French, Russian, Turk, Chinese, or African—simply as a man and therefore a possible heir of God through Christ. If that other man, no matter what his race or nation, be also a Christian, then the bond becomes mutual and therefore still stronger. "There is neither Jew nor Greek, there is neither slave nor free, there is neither male nor female; for you are all one in Christ Jesus."

It is for this reason that it is impossible for a Christian to engage in war. He knows no distinction of nationality, but regards all men as his brothers. The life of Christ is his life, for he is one with Christ. It would be as impossible for him to fight as it would be for Christ to have seized a sword and fought in self-defense when the Roman soldiers came for Him. And two Christians can no more fight against each other than Christ can fight against Himself.

However, we are not now engaged in discussing war, but are merely showing the absolute unity of believers in Christ. They are one. There is but one "Offspring," and that is Christ. However many millions of true believers there may be, they are one only in Christ. Each man has his own individuality, but it is in every case only the manifestation of some phase of the individuality of Christ. The human body has many members, and all members differ in their individuality. Yet there is absolute unity and harmony in every healthy body. With those who have put on the "new man," which is renewed in knowledge after the image of Him that created him, "there is neither Greek nor Jew, circumcision nor uncircumcision, Barbarian, Scythian, bond nor free; but Christ is all, and in all." Colossians 3:11, KJV.

The Harvest

In Christ's explanation of the parable of the tares and the wheat we are told that "the good seed [or offspring] means the sons of the kingdom." Matthew 13:38. The farmer would not allow the tares to be pulled out of the wheat because in the early stage it would be difficult to distinguish in every case between the wheat and the tares, and some of the wheat would be destroyed. So he said, "Let both grow together until the harvest; and at harvest time I will tell the reapers, Gather the weeds first and bind them in bundles to be burned, but gather the wheat into my barn." Verse 30. It is in the harvest that the seed is gathered. Everyone knows that.

But what the parable especially shows is that it is in the harvest that *the seed is fully manifested*. In short, that the seed comes *at harvesttime*. The harvest only waits for the seed to be fully manifested and matured.

But "the harvest is the end of the world." So the time when "the offspring should come to whom the promise had been made" (Galatians 3:19) is the end of the world, when the time comes for the promise of the new earth to be fulfilled. Indeed, the "offspring" or "seed" cannot possibly be said to come before that time.

Read now Galatians 3:19 that the law was spoken because of transgression "till the offspring should come to whom the promise had been made." What do we learn from that? Simply this: that the law as spoken from Sinai without the change of a single letter, is an integral part of the gospel and must be presented in the gospel until the second coming of Christ at the end of the world. "Till heaven and earth pass away, not an iota, not a dot will pass from the law." Matthew 5:18. And what of the time when heaven and earth pass and the new heaven and the new earth come? Then the law will not be needed written in a book for men to preach to sinners, showing them their sins. *It will be in the heart of every man.* Hebrews 8:10, 11. Done away? Not by any means. But indelibly engraved *in the heart* of every individual, written not with ink but with the Spirit of the living God.

The "offspring" refers to all who belong to Christ. And we know that Christ's "promised inheritance" has not yet come in its fullness. Jesus Christ on earth did not receive the promised "inheritance" any more than Abraham did. Christ cannot come into the "inheritance" until Abraham does, for the promise was "to Abraham *and* to his offspring." The Lord by Ezekiel spoke of the "inheritance" at the time when David ceased to have a representative on his throne on earth, and foretold the overthrow of Babylon, Persia, Greece, and Rome, in these words: "Remove the diadem, and take off the crown. … I will overturn, overturn, overturn it: and it shall be no more, until He come whose right it is; and I will give it Him." Ezekiel 21:26, 27, KJV.

So Christ sits on His Father's throne, "from henceforth *expecting* till His enemies be made His footstool." Hebrews 10:13, KJV. Soon will He come. Those who are led by the Spirit of God are the sons of God and joint heirs with Christ, so that Christ cannot come into the inheritance before they do. The "offspring" is one, not divided. When He comes to execute judgment and to slay those who choose to say, "We do not want this Man to reign over us" (Luke 19:14), He "comes in His glory, and all the angels with Him." Matthew 25:31.

Then will the "offspring" be complete, and the promise will be fulfilled. And until that time the law will faithfully perform its task of stirring up and pricking the consciences of sinners, giving them no rest until they become identified with Christ or cast Him off altogether. Do you accept the terms? Will you cease your complaints against the law which would save you from sinking into a fatal sleep? And will you in Christ accept its righteousness? Then, as Abraham's seed, and an heir according to the promise you can rejoice in your freedom from the bondage of sin, singing:

> "I'm a child of the King,
> A child of the King!
> With Jesus my Saviour,
> I'm a child of the King!"

CHAPTER 4

"Adoption as Sons"

¹ I mean that the heir, as long as he is a child, is no better than a slave, though he is the owner of all the estate; ² but he is under guardians and trustees until the date set by the father.

It must be apparent to all that the chapter division makes no difference in the subject. The third chapter closes with a statement as to *who* are the heirs, and the fourth chapter proceeds with a study of *how* we become heirs.

In Paul's time, although a child might have been heir to a vast estate, he had no more to do with it until he should come of age than did a servant (or slave). If he should never reach that age, then he would never actually enter upon his inheritance. So far as any share in the inheritance is concerned, he would have lived all his life as a servant.

³ So with us; when we were children, we were slaves to the elements of the world. ⁴ But when the time had fully come, God sent forth his Son, born of woman, born under the law, ⁵ to redeem those who were under the law, so that we might receive adoption as sons.

If we look at the fifth verse we see that "children" refers to the condition in which we find ourselves before we receive "the adoption as sons." It represents our condition before we were redeemed from the curse of the law, that is, before we were converted. It does not mean children of God as distinguished from worldlings, but the "children" of whom the apostle speaks in Ephesians 4:14 as "tossed to and fro and carried about with every wind of doctrine, by the cunning of men, by their craftiness in deceitful wiles." In short, it refers to us in our unconverted state, when we "were by nature the children of wrath, like the rest of mankind." Ephesians 2:3.

"When we were children" we were in bondage under the "elements of the world." "For all that is in the world, the lust of the flesh, and the lust of the eyes, and the pride of life, is not of the Father, but is of the world. And the world passeth away, and the lust thereof." 1 John 2:16, 17, KJV. The friendship of the world is enmity with God. "Whosoever therefore will be a friend of the world is the enemy of God." James 4:4, KJV. It is from "the present evil age" that Christ came to deliver us. We are warned to "beware lest any man spoil you through philosophy and vain deceit, after the tradition of men, after the rudiments of the world, and not after Christ." Colossians 2:8 KJV. The bondage to the "rudiments of the world" results from walking "according to the course of this world, ... in the lusts of our flesh, fulfilling the desires of the flesh and of the mind," being "by nature the children of wrath." Ephesians 2:1-3, KJV. It is the same bondage described in Galatians 3:22-24, "before faith came," when "we were confined under the law," under sin. It is the condition of men who are "without Christ, being aliens from the commonwealth of Israel, and strangers from the covenants of promise, having no hope, and without God in the world." Ephesians 2:12, KJV.

All Men, Possible Heirs

God has not cast off the human race. Since the first man created was called "the son of God," all men can also be heirs. "Before faith came," although all were wanderers from God, we were "under the law," guarded by a severe master, kept under restraint in order that we might be led to accept the promise. What a blessed thing it is that God counts even the ungodly, those who are in the bondage of sin, as His children, wandering, prodigal sons, but still children! God has made all men "accepted in the Beloved." Ephesians 1:6, KJV. This probationary life is given for the purpose of giving us a chance to acknowledge Him as Father and to become sons indeed. But unless we come back to Him we shall die as slaves of sin.

Christ came "when the time had fully come." A parallel statement in Romans 5:6 says: "While we were yet helpless, at the right time Christ died for the ungodly." But the death of Christ serves for those who live now and for those who lived before He was manifested in the flesh in Judea just as well as for the men who lived at that time. It had no more effect on the men of that generation. It is once for all and therefore has an equal effect on every age. "When the time had fully come" was the time foretold in prophecy when the Messiah should be revealed; but the redemption was for all men in *all* ages. He was foreordained before the foundation of the world, but was "*manifest* in these last times." 1 Peter 1:20, KJV. If it had been God's plan that He should have been revealed in this century or even not until the last year before the close of time, it would have made no difference with the gospel. "He ever liveth" (Hebrews 7:25, KJV) and He ever has lived, "the same yesterday and today and forever." (Hebrews 13:8) It is "through the eternal Spirit" that He offers Himself for us (Hebrews 9:14) so that the sacrifice is equally present and efficacious in every age.

"Born of a Woman"

God sent forth His Son, "born of woman," and, therefore, a real man. He lived and suffered all the ills and troubles that fall to the lot of man. "The Word became flesh," John 1:14. Christ always designated Himself as "the Son of man," thus forever identifying Himself with the whole human race. The bond of union can never be broken.

Being "born of woman," Christ was necessarily born "under the law," for such is the condition of all mankind. "In all things it behooved Him to be made like unto His brethren, that He might be a merciful and faithful High Priest in things pertaining to God, to make reconciliation for the sins of the people." Hebrews 2:17, KJV. He takes everything on Himself. "He has borne our griefs and carried our sorrows." Isaiah 53:4. "He took our infirmities and bore our diseases." Matthew 8:17. "All we like sheep have gone astray; we have turned everyone to his own way; and the Lord has laid on Him the iniquity of us all." Isaiah 53:6.

He redeems us by coming into our place literally and taking our load off our shoulders. "For our sake He made Him to be sin who knew no sin, so that in Him we might become the righteousness of God." 2 Corinthians 5:21.

In the fullest sense of the word and to a degree seldom thought of when the expression is used, He became man's substitute. That is, He identifies Himself so fully with us that everything that touches or affects us, touches and affects Him. "Not I, but Christ." We cast our cares on Him by humbling ourselves into the nothingness that we are and leaving our burden on Him alone.

Thus we see already how it is that He came "to redeem those who were under the law." He does it in the most practical and real way. Some suppose this expression to mean that Christ freed the Jews from the necessity of offering sacrifices or from any further obligation to keep the commandments. But if only the Jews were "under the law," then Christ came to redeem only the Jews. We must acknowledge that we are, or were before we believed, "under the law." For Christ came to redeem none but those who were under the law. To be "under the law," as we have already seen, means to be condemned to death by the law as transgressors. Christ did "not come to call the righteous, but sinners to repentance." Matthew 9:13, KJV. But the law condemns none but those who are accountable to it and ought to keep it. Since Christ redeems us from condemnation of the law, it follows that He redeems us to a life of obedience to it.

"That We Might Receive Adoption as Sons"

"Beloved, now are we the sons of God." 1 John 3:2, KJV. "As many as received Him, to them gave He power to become the sons of God, even to them that believe on His name." John 1:12, KJV. This is an altogether different state from that described in Galatians 4:3 as "children." In that state we were "a rebellious people, lying children, children that will not hear the law of the Lord." Isaiah 30:9, KJV. Believing on Jesus and receiving "adoption as sons," we are described "as obedient children not fashioning yourselves according to the former lusts in your ignorance." 1 Peter 1:14, KJV. Christ said, "I delight to do Thy will, O My God; Thy law is within My heart." Psalm 40:8. Therefore, since He becomes our substitute, literally taking our place, not *instead* of us, but coming *into* us and living His life *in* us and *for* us, it necessarily follows that the same law must be within our hearts when we receive the adoption of sons.

⁶ And because you are sons, God has sent the Spirit of his Son into our hearts, crying, "Abba! Father!" ⁷ So through God you are no longer a slave but a son, and if a son then an heir.

Oh, what joy and peace come with the entering of the Spirit into the heart as a permanent resident, not as a guest but as sole proprietor! "Being justified by faith, we have peace with God through our Lord Jesus Christ," so that we rejoice even in tribulations, having hope that never disappoints, "because the love of God is shed abroad in our hearts by the Holy Ghost, which is given unto us." Romans 5:1, 5, KJV. Then we can love even as God does because we share in His divine nature. "The Spirit Himself" bears "witness with our spirit that we are children of God." Romans 8:16.

Just as there are two kinds of "children," so there are two classes of "slaves." While "children of wrath," men are slaves to sin, not servants of God. The Christian is a "servant"—a servant of God; but he serves in a far different manner from that in which the slave of sin serves Satan. The character of the servant depends on the master whom he serves.

In this chapter the word "slave" invariably applies not to servants of God but to the slaves of sin. Between the slave of sin and a son of God there is a vast difference. The slave can possess nothing and has no control over himself. This is his distinguishing characteristic. The freeborn son, on the contrary, was given dominion over every created thing as in the beginning, because he was united with God.

When the prodigal son was wandering from the father's house, he was "no better than a slave," because he was doing the most menial drudgery. In that condition he came back to the old homestead, feeling that he deserved no better place than that of a servant. But the father received him as a son, even though he had forfeited all right to sonship.

We have also forfeited our right to be called "sons." We have squandered away the inheritance. But God receives us back in Christ as sons indeed. He gives us the same rights and privileges Christ has. Although Christ is now in heaven at the right hand of God, "far above all principality, and power, and might, and dominion, and every name that is named, not only in this world, but also in that which is to come" (Ephesians 1:21, KJV), He shares His inheritance with us.

"God, who is rich in mercy, for His great love wherewith He loved us, even when we were dead in sins, hath quickened us [made us alive] together with Christ. … and hath raised us up together, and made us sit together in heavenly places in Christ." Ephesians 2:4-6, KJV. Christ is one with us in our present suffering, that we may be one with Him in His present glory. He has "exalted those of low degree." Luke 1:52. Even now, "He raises up the poor from the dust; He lifts the needy from the ash heap, to make them sit with princes and inherit a seat of honor." 1 Samuel 2:8. No king on earth has so great possessions or so much actual power as the poorest peasant who knows the Lord as his Father.

8 Formerly, when you did not know God, you were in bondage to beings that by nature are no gods;

Writing to the Corinthians, Paul said, "You know that when you were heathen, you were led astray to dumb idols." 1 Corinthians 12:2. Even so it was with the Galatians. They had been heathen, worshiping idols, and in bondage to the most degrading superstitions.

This bondage is the same as the bondage referred to in the preceding chapter—being "confined under the law." This is the same bondage in which all unconverted persons find themselves. In the second and third chapters of Romans we are told that "there is no difference; for *all* have sinned." The Jews themselves who did not know the Lord by personal experience were in the same bondage, the bondage of sin. "Everyone who commits sin is *of the devil.*" 1 John 3:8. "What pagans sacrifice they offer to demons and not to God." 1 Corinthians 10:20. If a man is not a Christian, he is a heathen; there is no middle ground. If the Christian apostatizes, he becomes a heathen.

We ourselves once walked "according to the course of this world, according to the prince of the power of the air, the spirit that now worketh in the children of disobedience." Ephesians 2:2, KJV. "Were once foolish, disobedient, led astray, slaves to various passions and pleasures, passing our days in malice and envy, hated by men and hating one another." Titus 3:3. We were "in bondage to beings that by nature are no gods." The crueler the master, the worse the bondage! What language can depict the horror of being in bondage to corruption itself?

⁹ but now that you have come to know God, or rather to be known by God, how can you turn back again to the weak and beggarly elements, whose slaves you want to be once more?

Is it not strange that men should be in love with chains? Christ has proclaimed "liberty to the captives, and the opening of the prison to those who are bound" (Isaiah 61:1), "saying to the prisoners, 'Come forth,' and to those who are in darkness, 'Appear.'" (Isaiah 49:9). Yet some who have heard these words and have come out and seen the light of "the Sun of Righteousness" and tasted the sweets of liberty, actually turn round and go back into their prison. They want to be bound with their old chains, even fondling them, and labor away at the hard treadmill of sin. It is no beautiful picture. Men can come to love the most revolting things, even death itself. What a vivid picture of human experience!

¹⁰ You observe days, and months, and seasons, and years! ¹¹ I am afraid I have labored over you in vain.

There is just as much danger for us in this respect as there ever was for the Galatians. Whoever trusts in himself is worshiping the works of his own hands instead of God, just as truly as does anyone who makes and bows down to a graven image. It is so easy for a man to trust his own supposed shrewdness, his ability to take care of himself, and to forget that the thoughts even of the wise are vain, and that there is no power but of God. "Let not the wise man glory in his wisdom, neither let the mighty man glory in his might, let not the rich man glory in his riches; but let him that glorieth glory in this, that he understandeth and knoweth Me, that I am the Lord which exercise loving-kindness, judgment, and righteousness, in the earth: for in these things I delight, saith the Lord." Jeremiah 9:23, 24, KJV.

¹² Brethren, I beseech you, become as I am, for I also have become as you are. You did me no wrong; ¹³ you know it was because of a bodily ailment that I preached the gospel to you at first; ¹⁴ and though my condition was a trial to you, you did not scorn or despise me, but received me as an angel of God, as Christ Jesus. ¹⁵ What has become of the satisfaction you felt? For I bear you witness that, if possible, you would have

plucked out your eyes and given them to me. [16] Have I then become your enemy by telling you the truth? [17] They make much of you, but for no good purpose; they want to shut you out, that you may make much of them. [18] For a good purpose it is always good to be made much of, and not only when I am present with you. [19] My little children, with whom I am again in travail until Christ be formed in you! [20] I could wish to be present with you now and to change my tone, for I am perplexed about you.

The apostle Paul was sent by God and the Lord Jesus Christ, and he delivered a message from God, not man. The work was God's. He was but the humble instrument, the "earthen vessel," which God had chosen as the means of carrying His glorious gospel of grace. Therefore, Paul did not feel affronted when his message was unheeded or even rejected. "Ye have not injured me at all" (KJV), he says. He did not regret the labor that he had bestowed upon the Galatians as though it were so much of his time wasted; but he was fearful for them, lest his labor had been in vain as far as they were concerned.

The man who from the heart can say, "Not unto us, O Lord, not unto us, but unto Thy name give glory, for Thy mercy, and for Thy truth's sake" (Psalm 115:1, KJV), cannot feel personally injured if his message is not received. Whoever becomes irritated when his teaching is slighted or ignored or scornfully rejected shows either that he has forgotten that it was God's words that he was speaking, or else that he had mingled with them or substituted for them words of his own.

In the past this personal pride has led to persecutions that have disgraced the professed Christian church. Men have arisen speaking perverse things to draw away disciples after themselves. When their sayings and customs were not heeded, they have been offended and have exercised their vengeance on the so-called "heretics." The dedicated person should frequently ask himself, *Whose servant am I?* If God's, then he will be content with delivering the message that God has given him, leaving vengeance to God to whom it belongs.

Paul's "Bodily Ailment"

From the incidental statements in this letter we can gather tidbits of history. Having been detained in Galatia by physical weakness, Paul preached the gospel "in demonstration of the Spirit and power" (1 Corinthians 2:4), so that the people saw

Christ crucified among them and, accepting Him, were filled with the power and joy of the Holy Ghost. Their joy and blessedness in the Lord were testified to publicly, and they suffered much persecution in consequence. But this they counted as nothing. In spite of his "weak" appearance (compare 1 Corinthians 2:1-5 and 2 Corinthians 10:10), they received Paul as God's own messenger because of the joyful news that he brought. So highly did they appreciate the riches of grace which he had opened up to them that they would gladly have given their own eyes to supply his deficiency.

This Paul mentions in order that the Galatians may see where they have fallen, and that they may know that the apostle was sincere. He told them the truth once, and they rejoiced in it; it is not possible that he is become their enemy because he continues to tell them the same truth.

But there is still more in these personal references. We must not imagine that Paul was pleading for personal sympathy when he referred to his afflictions and to the great inconvenience under which he had labored. Far from it. Not for a moment did he lose sight of the purpose for which he was writing, namely, to show that "the flesh profiteth nothing" and everything good is from the Holy Spirit of God. The Galatians had "begun in the Spirit." Paul was naturally small of stature and apparently weak in body. Furthermore, he was suffering a special affliction when he first met them. Yet he preached the gospel with such mighty power that none could fail to see that there was a real, although unseen, Presence with him. The gospel is not of man, but of God.

It was not made known to them by the flesh, and they were not indebted to the flesh for any of the blessings that they had received. What blindness, what infatuation, then, for them to think to perfect by their own efforts that which nothing but the power of God could begin! Have we learned this lesson?

"What Has Become of the Satisfaction You Felt?"

Everyone who has ever had any acquaintance with the Lord knows that in accepting Him there is joy. It is always expected that a new convert will have a beaming countenance and a joyful testimony. So it had been with the Galatians. But now their expressions of thanksgiving had given way to bickering and strife. The first joy and the warmth of the first love was gradually dying away. This was not as it should have been. "The path of the just is as the shining light, that shineth more and more unto the perfect day." Proverbs 4:18, KJV. The just live by faith. When men turn from the faith or attempt to substitute works for it, the light goes out. Jesus said, "These things have I spoken unto you, that My joy might *remain* in you, and that your joy might be full." John 15:11, KJV. The fountain of life is never exhausted. The supply is never diminished. If therefore our light grows dim and our joy gives place to a dull, monotonous grind, we may know that we have turned aside out of the way of life.

²¹ Tell me, you who desire to be under law, do you not hear the law? ²² For it is written that Abraham had two sons, one by a slave and one by a free woman. ²³ But the son of the slave was born according to the flesh, the son of the free woman through promise. ²⁴ Now this is an allegory: these women are two covenants. One is from Mount Sinai, bearing children for slavery; she is Hagar. ²⁵ Now Hagar is Mount Sinai in Arabia; she corresponds to the present Jerusalem, for she is in slavery with her children. ²⁶ But the Jerusalem above is free, and she is our mother. ²⁷ For it is written,

> **"Rejoice, O barren one who does not bear;**
> **break forth and shout, you who are not in travail;**
> **for the children of the desolate one are many more**
> **than she which hath an husband."**

How many there are who love ways that everybody but themselves can see are leading them directly to death. With their eyes wide open to the consequences of their course, they persist, deliberately choosing "the pleasures of sin for a season," rather than righteousness and length of days. To be "under the law" of God is to be condemned by it as a sinner, chained and doomed to death. Yet many millions besides the Galatians have loved the condition and still love it. If they would only hear what the law says! There is no reason why they should not, for it speaks in thunder tones. "He who has ears to hear, let him hear." Matthew 11:15.

It says, "Cast out the slave and her son; for the son of the slave shall not inherit with the son of the free woman," Verse 30. It speaks death to all who take pleasure in the "beggarly elements" of the world. "Cursed be everyone who does not abide by all things written in the book of the law, and do them." Galatians 3:10. The poor slave is to be cast out "into outer darkness: there shall be weeping and gnashing of teeth." Matthew 25:30, KJV. "For, behold, the day cometh, that shall burn as an oven; and all the proud, yea, and all that do wickedly, shall be stubble; and the day that cometh shall burn them up, saith the Lord of hosts, that it shall leave them neither root nor branch." Therefore, "Remember ye the law of Moses My servant, which I commanded unto him in Horeb for all Israel, with the statutes and judgments." Malachi 4:1, 4, KJV. All who are "under the law," whether they be called Jews or Gentiles, Christians or heathen, are in bondage to Satan—in the bondage of transgression and sin—and are to be "cast out." "Everyone who commits sin is a slave to sin. The slave does not continue in the house forever; the son continues forever." John 8:34, 35. Thank God, then, for "adoption as sons."

False teachers would persuade the brethren that in turning from wholehearted faith in Christ and trusting to works which they themselves could do, they would become children of Abraham and so heirs of the promises. "They which are the children of the flesh, these are not the children of God; but the children of the promise are counted for the seed." Romans 9:8, KJV. Now, of the two sons of Abraham, one was born after the flesh, and the other was by "promise," born of the Spirit. "By faith Sarah herself received power to conceive, even when she was past the age, since she considered Him faithful who had promised." Hebrews 11:11.

Hagar was an Egyptian slave. The children of a slave woman are slaves, even though their father is free. So Hagar could bring forth children only to bondage.

But long before the servant-child Ishmael was born, the Lord had plainly signified to Abraham that his own free son, born of his free wife Sarah, would inherit the promise. Such are the workings of the Almighty.

"These Women Are Two Covenants"

The two women, Hagar and Sarah, represent the two covenants. We read that Hagar is Mount Sinai, "bearing children for slavery." Just as Hagar could bring forth only slave children, so the law, even the law that God spoke from Sinai, cannot beget free men. It can do nothing but hold them in bondage. "The law brings wrath," "since through the law comes knowledge of sin." Romans 4:15; 3:20. At Sinai the people promised to keep the given law. But in their own strength they had no power to keep the law. Mount Sinai "bore children for slavery," since their promise to make themselves righteous by their own works was not successful and can never be.

Consider the situation: The people were in the bondage of sin. They had no power to break their chains. And the speaking of the law made no change in that condition. If a man is in prison for crime, he does not gain release by hearing the statutes read to him. Reading to him the law that put him there only makes his captivity more painful.

Then did not God Himself lead them into bondage? Not by any means, since He did not induce them to make that covenant at Sinai. Four hundred and thirty years before that time He had made a covenant with Abraham which was sufficient for all purposes. That covenant was confirmed in Christ, and therefore was a covenant from above. See John 8:23. It promised righteousness as a free gift of God through faith, and it included all nations. All the miracles that God had wrought in delivering the children of Israel from Egyptian bondage were but demonstrations of His power to deliver them (and us) from the bondage of sin. Yes, the deliverance from Egypt was itself a demonstration not only of God's power but also of His desire to lead them from the bondage of sin.

So, when the people came to Sinai, God simply referred them to what He had already done and then said, "Now therefore, if ye will obey My voice indeed, and keep My covenant, then ye shall be a peculiar treasure unto Me above all people: for all the earth is Mine." Exodus 19:5, KJV. To what covenant did He refer? Evidently to the one already in existence, His covenant with Abraham. If they would simply keep *God's* covenant, keep the faith, and believe God's promise, they would be a "peculiar treasure" unto God. As the possessor of all the earth, He was able to do for them all that He had promised.

The fact that they in their self-sufficiency rashly took the whole responsibility upon themselves does not prove that God had led them into making that covenant.

If the children of Israel who came out of Egypt had but walked "in the steps of that faith of our father Abraham" (Romans 4:12, KJV), they would never have boasted that they could keep the law spoken from Sinai, "for the promise, that he should be the heir of the world, was not to Abraham, or to his seed, through the law, but through the righteousness of faith." (Romans 4:13, KJV). Faith justifies. Faith makes righteous. If the people had had Abraham's faith, they would have had the righteousness that he had. At Sinai the law, which was "spoken because of transgression," would have been in their *hearts*. They would not have needed to be awaked by its thunders to a sense of their condition. God never expected, and does not now expect, that any person can get righteousness by the law proclaimed from Sinai, and everything connected with Sinai shows it. Yet the law is truth and must be kept. God delivered the people from Egypt "that they might observe His statutes, and keep His laws." Psalm 105:45, KJV. We do not get life by keeping the commandments, but God gives us life in order that we may keep them through faith in Him.

The Two Covenants Parallel

The apostle when speaking of Hagar and Sarah says: "These women are two covenants." These two covenants exist today. The two covenants are not matters of time, but of condition. Let no one flatter himself that he cannot be bound under the old covenant, thinking that its time has passed. The time for that is passed only in the sense that "the time past of our life may suffice us to have wrought the will of the Gentiles, when we walked in lasciviousness, lusts, excess of wine, revelings, banquetings, and abominable idolatries." 1 Peter 4:3, KJV.

The difference is just the difference between a free woman and a slave. Hagar's children, no matter how many she might have had, would have been slaves while those of Sarah would necessarily be free. So the covenant from Sinai holds all who adhere to it in bondage "under the law," while the covenant from above gives freedom, not freedom from obedience to the law, but freedom from disobedience to it. The freedom is not found away from the law but in the law. Christ redeems from the curse, which is the transgression of the law, so that the blessing may come on us. And the blessing is obedience to the law. "Blessed are those whose way is blameless, who *walk in the law of the Lord.*" Psalm 119:1. *This blessedness is freedom.* "I shall walk at liberty; for I have sought Thy precepts." Psalm 119:45.

The difference between the two covenants may be put briefly thus: In the covenant from Sinai we ourselves have to do with the law alone, while in the covenant from above we have the law in Christ. In the first instance it is death to us, since the law is sharper than any two-edged sword, and we are not able to handle it without fatal results. But in the second instance we have the law "in the hand of a Mediator." In the one case it is what *we* can do. In the other case it is what *the Spirit of God* can do.

Bear in mind that there is not the slightest question in the whole letter to the Galatians as to whether or not the law should be kept. The only question is: *How* shall it be kept? Is it to be our own doing, so that the reward shall not be of grace but of debt? Or is it to be God working in us both to will and to do of His good pleasure?

Mount Sinai vs. Mount Zion

As there are the two covenants, so there are two cities to which they pertain. Jerusalem which now is pertains to the old covenant—to Mount Sinai. It will never be free but will be replaced by the City of God, the heavenly Jerusalem, which comes down out of heaven. Revelation 3:12; 21:1-5. It is the city for which Abraham looked, the "city which has foundations, whose builder and maker is God." Hebrews 11:10. Compare Revelation 21:14, 19, 20.

There are many who build great hopes—all their hopes—on the present Jerusalem. For such "to this day, when they read the old covenant, that same veil remains unlifted." 2 Corinthians 3:14. They are in reality looking to Mount Sinai and the old covenant for salvation. But it is not to be found there. "For ye are not come unto the mount that might be touched, and that burned with fire, nor unto blackness, and darkness, and tempest, and the sound of a trumpet, and the voice of words; ... but ye are come unto Mount Zion, and unto the city of the living God, the heavenly Jerusalem, ... and to Jesus the Mediator of the new covenant, and to the blood of sprinkling, that speaketh better things than that of Abel." Hebrews 12:18-24, KJV. Whoever looks to the present Jerusalem for blessings is looking to the old covenant, to Mount Sinai, to slavery. But whoever worships with his face toward the New Jerusalem, he who expects blessings only from it, is looking to the new covenant, to Mount Zion, and to freedom; for "Jerusalem above is free." From what is it free? Free from sin; and since it is our "mother," it begets us anew so that we also become free from sin. Free from the law? Yes, certainly, for the law has no condemnation for those who are in Christ Jesus.

But do not let anyone deceive you with vain words, telling you that you may now trample underfoot that law which God Himself proclaimed in such awful majesty from Sinai. Coming to Mount Zion, to Jesus, the Mediator of the new covenant, and to the blood of sprinkling, we become free from sin, from transgression of the law. The basis of God's throne in "Zion" is His law. From the throne proceed the same lightnings and thunderings and voices (Revelation 4:5; 11:19) as from Sinai, because the selfsame law is there. But it is "the throne of grace" (Hebrews 4:16), and therefore in spite of the thunders we come to it boldly, assured that from God we shall obtain mercy. We shall also find grace to help in time of need, grace to help us in the hour of temptation to sin, for out of the midst of the throne, from the slain Lamb (Revelation 5:6), flows the river of water of life bringing to us from the heart of Christ "the law of the Spirit of life." Romans 8:2. We drink of it, we bathe in it, and we find cleansing from all sin.

Why didn't the Lord bring the people directly to Mount Zion, then, where they could find the law as life, and not to Mount Sinai where it was only death?

That is a very natural question, and one that is easily answered. It was because of their unbelief. When God brought Israel out of Egypt, it was His purpose to bring them to Mount Zion as directly as they could go. When they had crossed the Red Sea, they sang an inspired song, of which this was a part: "Thou in Thy mercy hast led forth the people which Thou hast redeemed: Thou hast guided them in Thy strength unto Thy holy habitation. … Thou shalt bring them in, and plant them in the mountain of Thine inheritance, in the place, O Lord, which Thou hast made for Thee to dwell in, in the sanctuary, O Lord, which Thy hands have established." Exodus 15:13, 17, KJV.

If they had continued singing, they would very soon have come to Zion. For the redeemed of the Lord "come to Zion with singing, with everlasting joy upon their heads." Isaiah 35:10. The dividing of the Red Sea was the proof of this. See Isaiah 51:10, 11. But they soon forgot the Lord and murmured in unbelief. Therefore the law "was added because of transgressions." Galatians 3:19. It was their own fault—the result of their sinful unbelief—that they came to Mount Sinai instead of to Mount Zion.

Nevertheless, God did not leave Himself without witness of

His faithfulness. At Mount Sinai the law was in the hand of the same Mediator, Jesus, to whom we come when we come to Zion. From the rock in Horeb (which is Sinai) flowed the living stream, the water of life from the heart of Christ. See Exodus 17:6; 1 Corinthians 10:4. There they had the reality of Mount Zion. Every soul whose heart there turned to the Lord would have beheld His unveiled glory, even as Moses did, and being transformed by it would have found the ministration of righteousness, instead of the ministration of condemnation. "His mercy endureth forever," and even upon the clouds of wrath from which proceed the thunders and lightnings of the law shines the glorious face of the Sun of Righteousness and forms the bow of promise.

28 Now we, brethren, like Isaac, are children of promise. 29 But as at that time he who was born according to the flesh persecuted him who was born according to the Spirit, so it is now. 30 But what does the Scripture say? "Cast out the slave and her son; for the son of the slave shall not inherit with the son of the free woman." 31 So, brethren, we are not children of the slave but of the free woman.

Here is comfort for every soul! You are a sinner, or at best trying to be a Christian, and you tremble in terror at these words, "Cast out the slave." You realize that you are a slave, that sin has a hold upon you and you are bound by the cords of evil habits. You must learn not to be afraid when the Lord speaks, for He speaks peace even though it be with a voice of thunder! The more majestic the voice, the greater the peace that He gives. Take courage!

The son of the bondwoman is the flesh and its works. "Flesh and blood cannot inherit the kingdom of God, nor does the perishable inherit the imperishable." 1 Corinthians 15:50. But God says, "Cast out the slave and her son." If you are willing that His will shall be done in you "as it is in heaven," He will see that the flesh and its works are cast out from you and you will be "delivered from the bondage of corruption into the glorious liberty of the children of God." Romans 8:21, KJV. That command which so frightened you is simply the voice commanding the evil spirit to depart and to come no more into you. It speaks to you victory over every sin. Receive Christ by faith, and you have the power to become the son of God, heir of a kingdom which cannot be moved, but which with all its people abides forever.

"Stand Fast Therefore." Galatians 5:1.

Where shall we stand? In the freedom of Christ Himself, whose delight was in the law of the Lord because it was in His heart. See Psalm 40:8. "The law of the Spirit of life in Christ Jesus has set me free from the law of sin and death." Romans 8:2. We stand only by faith.

In this freedom there is no trace of bondage. It is perfect liberty. It is liberty of soul, liberty of thought, as well as liberty of action. It is not that we are simply given the ability to keep the law, but we are given the mind that finds delight in doing it. It is not that we comply with the law because we see no other way of escape from punishment; that would be galling bondage. It is from such bondage that God's covenant releases us.

No, the promise of God when accepted puts the mind of the Spirit into us so that we find the highest pleasure in obedience to all the precepts of God's Word. The soul is as free as a bird soaring above the mountaintops. It is the glorious liberty of the children of God, who have the full range of the breadth, and length, and depth, and height of God's universe. It is the liberty of those who do not have to be watched but who can be trusted anywhere, since their every step is but the movement of God's own holy law. Why be content with slavery when such limitless freedom is yours? The prison doors are open; walk out into God's freedom.

CHAPTER 5

The Spirit Makes It Easy to be Saved

¹ For freedom Christ has set us free; stand fast therefore, and do not submit again to a yoke of slavery.

The connection between the fourth and fifth chapters of Galatians is close, so much so that it is difficult to see how anybody could ever have hit upon the idea of making a chapter division.

The Freedom That Christ Gives

When Christ was manifest in the flesh His work was "to proclaim liberty to the captives, and the opening of the prison to those who are bound." Isaiah 61:1. The miracles that He performed were practical illustrations of this work, and one of the most striking may well be considered just now.

"And He was teaching in one of the synagogues on the Sabbath. And, behold there was a woman which had a spirit of infirmity eighteen years, and was bowed together, and could in no wise lift up herself. And when Jesus saw her, He called her to Him, and said unto her, Woman, thou art loosed from thine infirmity. And He laid His hands on her; and immediately she was made straight, and glorified God." Luke 13:10-13, KJV.

Then when the hypocritical ruler of the synagogue complained because Jesus did this miracle on the Sabbath, He referred to how each one would loose his ox or ass from the stall, and lead him to water; then He said:

"And ought not this woman, being a daughter of Abraham, whom Satan hath bound, lo, these eighteen years, be loosed from this bond on the Sabbath day?" Verse 16.

Two features in this case are worthy of special note: the woman was bound by Satan; and she had "a spirit of infirmity," or absence of strength.

Now note how accurately this describes our condition before we meet Christ;

(1) We are bound by Satan, "captured by him to do his will," 2 Timothy 2:26. "Everyone who commits sin is the slave of sin" (John 8:34), and "he who commits sin is of the devil" (1 John 3:8). "His own iniquities shall take the wicked himself, and he shall be holden with the cords of his sins." Proverbs 5:22, KJV. Sin is the cord with which Satan binds us.

(2) We have "a spirit of infirmity," and can in no wise lift ourselves up or free ourselves from the chains that bind us. It was when we were "without strength" that Christ died for us. Romans 5:6, KJV. These two words, "without strength," are translated from the very same word that is rendered "infirmity" in the story of the woman whom Jesus healed. She was "without strength." That is our condition.

What does Jesus do for us? He takes the weakness and gives us in return His strength. "We have not an high priest which cannot be touched with the feeling of our infirmities." Hebrews 4:15, KJV. "Himself took our infirmities, and bare our sicknesses." Matthew 8:17, KJV. He becomes all that we are, in order that we may become all that He is. He was "born under the law, to redeem those who were under the law." Galatians 4:4, 5. He has delivered us from the curse, being made a curse for us, that the blessing might come to us. Although He knew no sin, He was made to be sin for us, "so that in Him we might become the righteousness of God." 2 Corinthians 5:21.

Why did Jesus make that woman free from her infirmity? In order that she might walk at liberty. Certainly it was not in order that she might continue of her own free will to do that which before she was obliged to do. And why does He make us free from sin? In order that we may *live* free from sin. On account of the weakness of our flesh we are unable to do the righteousness of the law. Therefore Christ, who is come in the flesh and who has power over all flesh, strengthens us. He gives us His mighty Spirit that the righteousness of the law may be fulfilled in us. In Christ we walk not after the flesh but after the Spirit. We cannot tell how He does it. He alone knows how it is done, because He alone has the power. But we may know its reality.

While she was yet bound down and unable to lift herself up, Jesus said to the woman, "Thou art loosed from thine infirmity." "Thou art loosed"—*Present tense*. That is just what He says to us. To every captive He has proclaimed deliverance.

The woman "could in no wise lift up herself," yet at the word of Christ she at once stood erect. She could not do it, yet she did. The things that are impossible for men are possible for God. "The Lord upholds all who are falling, and raises up all who are bowed down." Psalm 145:14. Faith does not make facts. It only lays hold of them. There is not a single soul that is bowed down with the weight of sin which Satan has bound on him, whom Christ does not lift up. Freedom is his. He has only to *make use* of it. Let the message be sounded far and wide. Let every soul hear it, that Christ has given deliverance to every captive. Thousands will rejoice at the news.

Christ came to restore that which was lost. He redeems us from the curse. He has redeemed us. Therefore the liberty wherewith He makes us free is the liberty that existed before the curse came. Man was made king over the earth. It was not merely the one individual first created who was made king, but all mankind. "In the day that God created man, in the likeness of God made He him; male and female created He them; and blessed them, and called their name Adam," that is, man. Genesis 5:1, 2, KJV. "And God said, let Us make man in Our image, after Our likeness; and let them have dominion over the fish of the sea, and over the fowl of the air, and over the cattle, and over all the earth and over every creeping thing that creepeth upon the earth. So God created man in His own image, in the image of God created He him; male and female created He them. And God blessed them, and God said unto them, Be fruitful, and multiply, and replenish the earth, and subdue it; and have dominion." Genesis 1:26-28, KJV. The dominion, we see, was given *to every human being*, male and female.

When God made man, He put "everything in subjection under his feet." Hebrews 2:8. It is true that now we do not see all things put under man. "But we see Jesus, who was made a little lower than the angels, for the suffering of death, crowned with glory and honour; that He by the grace of God should taste death for every man." Hebrews 2:9, KJV. Thus He redeems every man from the curse of the lost dominion. A crown implies kingship, and Christ's crown is that which man had when he was set over the works of God's hands. Accordingly, Christ (as a man, in the flesh), just as He was about to ascend to heaven after the resurrection, said: "All power is given unto Me in heaven and in earth. Go ye therefore." Matthew 28:18, 19, KJV. This indicates that the same power once lost through sin, is given to us in Him.

Christ has tasted death for us as a man and through the cross has redeemed us from the curse. If we are crucified with Him, we are also risen with Him and made to sit together with Him in the heavenly places, with all things under our feet. If we do not know this, it is only because we have not allowed the Spirit to reveal it to us. The eyes of our heart need to be enlightened by the Spirit that we may know "what is the hope to which He has called you, what are the riches of His glorious inheritance in the saints." Ephesians 1:18.

The exhortation to those who are dead and risen with Christ is, "Let not sin therefore reign in your mortal bodies, to make you obey their passions." Romans 6:12. In Christ we have authority over sin, that it shall have no dominion over us.

When He "washed us from our sins in His own blood," He "made us kings and priests unto God and His Father." Revelation 1:5, 6, KJV. Glorious dominion! Glorious freedom! Freedom from the power of the curse, even while surrounded by it! Freedom from this present evil world, the lust of the flesh, the lust of the eyes, and the pride of life! Neither "the prince of the power of the air" (Ephesians 2:2) nor the "world rulers of this present darkness" (6:12) can have any dominion over us! It is the freedom and authority that Christ had when He said, "Begone, Satan." Matthew 4:10. And the devil immediately left Him.

It is such freedom that nothing in heaven or earth can coerce us to do anything against our will. God will not attempt it, for we hold our freedom from Him. And no one else can do it. It is power over the worldly principles, so that they will serve us instead of controlling us. We shall learn to recognize Christ and His cross everywhere, so that the curse will be powerless over us. Our health will "spring forth speedily," for the life of Jesus will be manifest in our mortal flesh. Such glorious liberty no tongue or pen can describe.

"Stand Fast"

"By the word of the Lord were the heavens made; and all the host of them by the breath of His mouth." "He spake, and it was done; He commanded, and it stood fast." Psalm 33:6, 9, KJV. The same word that created the starry host speaks to us, "Stand fast!" It is not a command that leaves us as helpless as before, but one which carries the performance of the act with it. The heavens did not create themselves, but were brought into existence by the word of the Lord. Then let them be your teachers. "Lift up your eyes on high and see: who created these? He who brings out their host by number, calling them all by name; by the greatness of His might, and because He is strong in power not one is missing." Isaiah 40:26. "He gives power to the faint, and to him who has no might He increases strength." Isaiah 40:29.

2 Now I, Paul, say to you that if you receive circumcision, Christ will be of no advantage to you.

It should be understood that much more is involved than the mere rite of circumcision. This letter, which has so much to say about circumcision, has been preserved by the Lord for us and contains the gospel message for all time, even though circumcision as a rite is not a burning, living question now.

The question is how to obtain righteousness—salvation from sin—and the inheritance that comes with it. The fact is that it can be obtained only by faith—by receiving Christ into the heart and allowing Him to live His life in us. Abraham had this righteousness of God by faith of Jesus Christ, and God gave Him circumcision as a sign of that fact. It had a special meaning to Abraham, continually reminding him of his failure when he tried by means of the flesh to fulfill God's promise. The record of it serves the same purpose for us. It shows that "the flesh profiteth nothing" and is not therefore to be depended on. The mere fact of being circumcised did not make Christ of no advantage, for Paul was himself circumcised, and as a matter of expediency he had Timothy circumcised. Acts 16:1-3. But Paul did not count his circumcision or any other external thing of value (Philippians 3:4-7), and when it was proposed to circumcise Titus as a thing necessary to salvation he would not allow it. Galatians 2:3-5.

That which was to be only the *sign* of an already existing fact was taken by subsequent generations as the *means* of establishing the fact. Circumcision therefore stands in this letter as the symbol of all kinds of "work" done by men with the hope of obtaining righteousness. It is "the works of the flesh," as opposed to the Spirit.

Now the truth is stated that if a person does anything with the hope of being saved by it, that is, of getting salvation by his own work, Christ is "of no advantage to him." If Christ is not accepted as a complete Redeemer, He is not accepted at all. That is to say, if Christ is not accepted for what He is, He is rejected. He cannot be other than what He is. Christ does not share with any other person or thing the fact of being Saviour. Therefore, it is easy to see that if anyone were circumcised with the hope of receiving salvation thereby, it would show absence of faith in Christ as the all-sufficient and only Saviour of mankind.

God gave circumcision as a *sign* of faith in Christ. The Jews perverted it into a *substitute* for faith. So when a Jew boasted in his circumcision, he was boasting of his own righteousness. This is no disparagement of the law, but of man's ability to keep the law. It is the glory of the law that it is so holy and its requirements are so great that no man is able to attain to the perfection of it. Only in Christ is the righteousness of the law ours. True circumcision is to worship God in Spirit, to rejoice in Christ Jesus, and to put no confidence in the flesh. Philippians 3:3.

³ I testify again to every man who receives circumcision that he is bound to keep the whole law. ⁴ You are severed from Christ, you who would be justified by the law; you have fallen away from grace.

"There!" exclaims someone, "that shows that the law is a thing to be avoided, for Paul says that those who are circumcised have got to do the whole law and he warns them not to be circumcised."

Not quite so hasty, my friend. Stick a little more closely to the text. Notice the wording of verse 3 in the King James Version: "He is a *debtor* to do the whole law." You will see that the bad thing is not the law, nor the doing of the law, but being a debtor to the law. Is there not a vast difference? It is a good thing to have food to eat and clothes to wear, but it is a sorrowful thing to be in debt for these necessary things. Sadder yet is it to be in debt for them and yet to lack them.

A debtor is one who owes something. He who is in debt to the law owes what the law demands, namely, righteousness. Therefore whoever is in debt to the law is under the curse; for it is written, "Cursed be everyone who does not abide by all things written in the book of the law, and do them." Galatians 3:10. So to attempt to get righteousness by any other means than by faith in Christ is to incur the curse of eternal debt. He is eternally in debt, for he has nothing wherewith to pay. Yet the fact that he is in debt to the law—debtor to do the whole law—shows that he ought to do it all. *How* shall he do it? "This is the work of God, that you believe in Him whom He has sent." John 6:29. Let him cease trusting in himself and receive and confess Christ in his flesh, and then the righteousness of the law will be fulfilled in him because he will not walk after the flesh, but after the Spirit.

⁵ **For through the Spirit, by faith, we wait for the hope of righteousness.**

Don't pass this verse by without reading it more than once, or you will think that it says something that it does not say. And as you read it, think of what you have already learned about the promise of the Spirit.

Don't imagine that this verse teaches that having the Spirit we must *wait* for righteousness. Not by any means. The Spirit *brings* righteousness. "The Spirit *is* life because of righteousness." Romans 8:10, KJV. "When he comes, He will convince the world of sin and of righteousness." John 16:8. Whoever receives the Spirit has the conviction of sin and of the righteousness which the Spirit shows him that he lacks, and which the Spirit alone can bring.

What is the righteousness which the Spirit brings? It is the righteousness of the law. Romans 8:4. This we know, for "we know that the law is spiritual." Romans 7:14.

What, then, about the "hope of righteousness" for which we wait through the Spirit? Notice that it does not say that we through the Spirit hope *for* righteousness. Rather, we wait for the hope of righteousness by faith, that is, the hope which the possession of righteousness brings. Let us briefly go over this matter in detail to refresh our minds:

(1) The Spirit of God is, "the Holy Spirit of promise." The possession of the Spirit ensures to us the promise of God.

(2) That which God has promised to us as children of Abraham is an inheritance. The Holy Spirit is the pledge of this inheritance until the purchased possession is redeemed and bestowed upon us. Ephesians 1:13, 14.

(3) This inheritance that is promised is the new heavens and the new earth, in which righteousness dwells. 2 Peter 3:13.

(4) The Spirit brings righteousness. He is Christ's representative, the means by which Christ Himself, who is our righteousness, comes to dwell in our hearts. John 14:16-18.

(5) Therefore the hope which the Spirit brings is the hope of an inheritance in the kingdom of God, the earth made new.

(6) The righteousness which the Spirit brings to us is the righteousness of the law of God. Romans 8:4; 7:14. By the Spirit it is written in our hearts instead of on tables of stone. 2 Corinthians 3:3.

(7) The sum of the whole matter is this: If, instead of thinking ourselves so powerful that *we* can do the law, we will allow the Holy Spirit to come in that we may be filled with the righteousness of the law, we will have living hope dwelling in us. The hope of the Spirit— the hope of righteousness by faith—has no element of uncertainty in it. It is positive assurance. In nothing else is there any hope. He who does not have "the righteousness which is of God by faith" has no hope whatever. Only Christ in us is "the hope of glory."

⁶ For in Christ Jesus neither circumcision nor uncircumcision is of any avail, but faith working through love.

Circumcision is not able to do anything, neither is uncircumcision. Only faith, which works by love, can do anything. This faith which works by love is found only in Christ Jesus.

But what is it that there is talk about *doing*? Nothing else than the law of God. No man can do it, whatever his state or condition. The uncircumcised man has no power to keep the law, and circumcision has no power to enable him to do it. One may boast of his circumcision, and another may boast of his uncircumcision; but both are alike vain. By the principle of faith boasting is excluded. Romans 3:27. Since the faith of Christ alone can keep the righteousness of the law, there is no chance of us to tell what we have done. "All to Christ I owe."

⁷ You were running well; who hindered you from obeying the truth? ⁸ This persuasion is not from Him who calls you. ⁹ A little leaven leavens the whole lump. ¹⁰ I have confidence in the Lord that you will take no other view than mine; and he who is troubling you will bear his judgment, whoever he is. ¹¹ But if I, brethren, still preach circumcision, why am I still persecuted? In that case the stumbling block of the cross has been removed. ¹² I wish those who unsettle you would mutilate themselves!

God's law is the truth (Psalm 119:142), and the Galatian brethren had started out to obey it. They had succeeded in the beginning but later on had been hindered in their progress. "Why? Because they did not pursue it through faith, but as if it were based on works. They have stumbled over the stumbling stone." Romans 9:32. Christ is the way, the truth, and the life, and there is no stumbling in Him. The perfection of the law is in Him, for His life is the law.

The cross is and always has been a symbol of disgrace. To be crucified was to be subjected to the most ignominious death known. The apostle said that if he preached circumcision (that is, righteousness by works), "the offense of the cross" would cease. Galatians 5:11, KJV. The offense of the cross is that the cross is a confession of human frailty and sin and of inability to do any good thing. To take the cross of Christ means to depend solely on Him for everything, and this is the abasement of all human pride. Men love to fancy themselves independent. But let the cross be preached, let it be made known that in man dwells no good thing and that all must be received as a gift, and straightway somebody is offended.

¹³ For you were called to freedom, brethren; only do not use your freedom as an opportunity for the flesh, but through love be servants of one another. ¹⁴ For the whole law is fulfilled in one word, "You shall love your neighbor as yourself."

The two preceding chapters tell about bondage, imprisonment. Before faith comes we are "shut up" under sin, debtors to the law. The faith of Christ sets us free, but as we are set at liberty the admonition is given us, "Go, and sin no more," John 8:11, KJV. We have been set at liberty *from* sin, not at liberty *to* sin. How many make a mistake here!

Many sincere people imagine that in Christ we are at liberty to ignore and defy the law, forgetting that the transgression of the law is sin. 1 John 3:4. To serve the flesh is to commit sin, "because the carnal mind is enmity against God; for it is not subject to the law of God, neither indeed can be." Romans 8:7, KJV. The apostle warns us not to misuse the liberty which Christ gives us and bring ourselves into bondage again by transgressing the law. Instead of this, we should by love serve one another, for love is the fulfilling of the law.

Christ gives us the liberty of the first dominion. But remember that God gave the dominion to mankind, and that in Christ all are made kings. This shows that the only human being over whom any Christian has the right to rule is himself. The great man in Christ's kingdom is he who rules his own spirit.

As kings, we find our subjects in the lower orders of created beings, in the elements, and in our own flesh, but not in our fellowmen. We are to serve them. We are to have in us the mind that was in Christ while He was still in the royal court in heaven, "in the form of God," which led Him to take "the form of a servant." Philippians 2:5-7. This is further seen by the fact that He washed the feet of the disciples, with full consciousness of the fact that He was their Master and Lord and that He came from God and went to God. See John 13:3-13. Moreover, when all the redeemed saints appear in glory, Christ Himself "will gird Himself, and have them to sit at table, and He will come and serve them." Luke 12:37.

The greatest freedom is found in service—in service rendered to our fellows in the name of Jesus. He who does the greatest service (not greatest as men reckon, but what they would call lowest) is the greatest. This we learn from Christ who is King of kings and Lord of lords, because He is servant of all, performing service that nobody else would or could do. God's servants are all kings.

Love Fulfills the Law

Love is not a substitute for the keeping of the law, but is the perfection of it. "Love does no wrong to a neighbor; therefore love is the fulfilling of the law." Romans 13:10. "If anyone says, 'I love God,' and hates his brother, he is a liar; for he who does not love his brother whom he has seen, cannot love God whom he has not seen." 1 John 4:20. If a man loves his neighbor, it must be that he loves God. "Love is of God," for "God is love." Therefore love is the life of God. If that life is in us and is given free course, the law will necessarily be in us, for God's life is the law for all creation. "Hereby perceive we the love of God, because He laid down His life for us; and we ought to lay down our lives for the brethren." 1 John 3:16, KJV.

Love Is Unselfishness

Since love means service, the doing of something for others, it is evident that love takes no thought of itself. He who loves has no thought but of how he may bless others. So we read: "Love is patient and kind; love is not jealous or boastful; it is not arrogant or rude. Love does not insist on its own way; it is not irritable or resentful." 1 Corinthians 14:3, 5.

It is just on this vital point that many make a mistake. Happy are they who have found out their mistake and have come to the understanding and practice of true love. "Love seeketh not her own." Therefore self-love is not love at all, in the right sense of the word. It is only a base counterfeit. Yet most of that which in the world is called love is not really love for another, but is love of self.

Even that which should be the highest form of love known on earth, the love which is used by the Lord as a representation of His love for His people, the love of husband and wife, is more often selfishness than real love. Even leaving out marriages that are formed to gain wealth or position in society, in nearly every case the parties to a marriage are thinking more of their own individual happiness than of the happiness of the other. In proportion as real unselfish love exists, there is real happiness. It is a lesson that the world is slow to learn, that true happiness is found only when one ceases to seek for it and sets about making it for others.

"Love Never Ends"

Here again is a test which shows that much that is called love is not love. Love never ceases. The statement is absolute: *never*. There is no exception and no allowance made for circumstances. Love is not affected by circumstances. We often hear about one's love growing cold, but that is something that can never happen to true love. True love is always warm, always flowing; nothing can freeze the fountain of love. Love is absolutely endless and unchangeable, simply because it is the life of God. There is no other true love than the love of God, therefore the only possibility for true love to be manifested among mankind is for the love of God to be shed abroad in the heart by the Holy Spirit.

Sometime when a declaration of love is made, the loved one asks, "Why do you love me?" Just as if anybody could give a reason for love! Love is its own reason. If the lover can tell just why he loves another, that very answer shows that he does not really love. Whatever object he names as a reason for love may sometime cease to exist, and then his supposed love ceases. But "love never ends." Therefore love cannot depend upon circumstances. So the only answer that can be given to the question as to why one loves is "because"—because of love. Love loves, simply because it is love. Love is the quality of the individual who loves, and he loves because he has love, irrespective of the character of the object.

The truth of this is seen when we go back to God, the fountain of love. He is love. Love is His life. But no explanation of His existence can be given. The highest human conception of love is to love because we are loved, or because the object of our love is lovable. But God loves the *un*lovely. He loves those who hate Him. "For we ourselves were once foolish, disobedient, led astray, slaves to various passions and pleasures, passing our days in malice and envy, hated by men and hating one another; but when the goodness and lovingkindness of God our Saviour appeared, He saved us." Titus 3:3-5. "If you love those who love you, what reward have you? Do not even the tax collectors do the same?" "You, therefore, must be perfect, as your heavenly Father is perfect." Matthew 5:46, 48.

"Love does no wrong to a neighbor." The word "neighbor" means whoever dwells near. Love therefore extends to everything with which it comes in contact. He who loves must necessarily love everybody.

Since love does no wrong to his neighbor, it obviously follows that Christian love (and there is really no other true love, as we have seen) does not admit of wars and fightings. When the soldiers asked John the Baptist what they should do as followers of the Lamb of God to whom he pointed, he replied, "do violence to no man." Luke 3:14, KJV. An alternative rendering of John's answer is, "Put no man in fear." It would be a very mild war in which this command was followed! If an army were composed of Christians, true followers of Christ, when they came in contact with the enemy, instead of shooting them they would find out what they needed and supply their wants. "If thine enemy hunger, feed him; if he thirst, give him drink; for in so doing thou shalt heap coals of fire on his head. Be not overcome of evil, but overcome evil with good." Romans 12:20, 21, KJV.

15 But if you bite and devour one another take heed that you are not consumed by one another. 16 But I say, walk by the Spirit, and do not gratify the desires of the flesh. 17 For the desires of the flesh are against the Spirit, and the desires of the Spirit are against the flesh; for these are opposed to each other, to prevent you from doing what you would. 18 But if you are led by the Spirit you are not under the law.

By following evil counsel and departing from the simplicity of the faith, the Galatians were bringing themselves under the curse and in danger of hell. For "the tongue is a fire, a world of iniquity; so is the tongue among our members, that it defileth the whole body and setteth on fire the course of nature; and it is set on fire of hell." James 3:6, KJV. The tongue has devoured more than the sword, for the sword would never be drawn if it were not for the unruly tongue. No man can tame it, but God can. He had done it in the case of the Galatians when their mouths were filled with blessing and praise; but what a change had again taken place! As the result of their later instruction, they had descended from blessing to bickering. Instead of talking to edification, they were about to devour one another.

When there is bickering and strife in the church, be sure that the gospel has been sadly perverted. Let no one flatter himself on his orthodoxy or his soundness in the faith while he has a quarrelsome disposition or can be provoked to quarrel. Dissension and strife are the marks of departure from the faith, if one was ever in it. For, "since we are justified by faith, we have peace with God through our Lord Jesus Christ." Romans 5:1. We are not merely at peace with God, but we have peace with Him—His peace. So this new persuasion which led to strife and the devouring of one another with the tongue of unholy fire did not come from God, who had called them into the gospel. Only a step aside can eventually lead to a wide divergence. Two lines of railway may seem to lie parallel, yet insensibly they may diverge until they lead in opposite directions. "A little leaven leaveneth the whole lump." A seemingly little error, no matter what it be, has in it the germ of all wickedness. "Whosoever shall keep the whole law, and yet offend in one point, he is guilty of all." James 2:10, KJV. A single false principle adhered to will wreck the whole life and character. The little foxes spoil the vines.

[19] Now the works of the flesh are plain: fornication, impurity, licentiousness, [20] idolatry, sorcery, enmity, strife, jealousy, anger, selfishness, dissension, heresy, [21] envy, drunkenness, carousing, and the like. I warn you, as I warned you before, that those who do such things shall not inherit the kingdom of God.

Not a pleasant-sounding list, is it? But it is not all of them, for the apostle adds, "and the like." There is a good deal to think about in this list, taken in connection with the statement that "those who do such things shall not inherit the kingdom of God." Compare this list with that given by the Lord in Mark 7:21-23 as the things that come from within, from the heart of man. They belong to man by nature. Compare both these lists with the list given in Romans 1:28-32 as the things done by the heathen who did not like to retain God in their knowledge. They are the things that are done by all who do not know the Lord.

Then compare these lists of sins with the list given by the apostle Paul in 2 Timothy 3:1-5 of things that will be done in the last days by those who have only a "form of godliness." It will be noticed that all these lists are essentially the same. When men turn from the truth of the gospel, which is the power of God unto salvation to everyone who believes, they inevitably fall under the power of these sins.

"There Is No Difference"

There is only one flesh of man (1 Corinthians 15:39), since all the inhabitants of the earth are descendants of the one pair—Adam and Eve. "Sin came into the world through one man" (Romans 5:12), so that whatever sin there is in the world is common to all flesh. In the plan of salvation "there is no difference between the Jew and the Greek: for the same Lord over all is rich unto all that call upon Him." Romans 10:12, KJV. See also Romans 3:21-24. No person on earth can boast over another or has any right to despise another because of his sinful, degraded condition. The sight or knowledge of low vices in any people, instead of making us feel complacent over our superior morality, ought to fill us with sorrow and shame. It is but a reminder to us of what our human nature is. The works that manifest themselves in that murderer, that drunkard, or that libertine are simply the works of *our* flesh. The flesh of mankind has nothing else in its power but just such evil works as here described.

Some of the works of the flesh are generally recognized as very bad or, at any rate, as not respectable; but others are commonly regarded as paltry sins if not absolute virtues. Notice however the words "and the like," which indicate that all the things here named are identical in essence. The Scripture tells us that hatred is murder. "Anyone who hates his brother is a murderer." 1 John 3:15. Moreover, anger is also murder, as shown by the Saviour in Matthew 5:21, 22. Envy, which is so common also contains murder in it. But who regards envy as sinful? So far from being regarded as sinful in the extreme, it is cultivated throughout our society. And yet the word of God assures us that it is of the same kind as adultery, fornication, murder, and drunkenness, and that they which do such things shall not inherit the kingdom of God. Is it not a fearful thing?

The love of self, the desire for supremacy, is the source of all the other sins that are mentioned. Out of that have grown innumerable murders. The abominable works of the flesh are lurking where many least suspect them! They are wherever human flesh is and are manifest in some form or other wherever the flesh is not crucified. "Sin lieth at the door."

The Flesh and the Spirit in Conflict

The flesh and the Spirit of God have nothing in common. They are "opposed to each other," that is, they act against each other like two foes, each eagerly watching the opportunity to crush the other. The flesh is corruption. It cannot inherit the kingdom of God because corruption does not inherit incorruption. 1 Corinthians 15:50. The flesh cannot be converted. It must be crucified, "The carnal [fleshly] mind is enmity against God: for it is not subject to the law of God, neither indeed can be. So then they that are in the flesh cannot please God." Romans 8:7, 8, KJV.

Here is the secret of the backsliding of the Galatians and of the trouble which so many find in living the Christian life. The Galatians began in the Spirit, but thought to attain to perfection by the flesh (chapter 3:3), a thing as impossible as to reach the stars by delving in the earth. So many people desire to do right; but not having definitely and fully yielded to the Spirit, they cannot do the things that they would. The Spirit strives with them and has partial control, or is at times quite fully yielded to, and they have a rich experience. Then the Spirit is grieved, the flesh asserts itself, and they seem like other persons. They are swayed at times by the mind of the Spirit and at times by the mind of the flesh (Romans 8:6); and so, being double-minded, they are unstable in all their ways (James 1:8). It is a most unsatisfactory position in which to be.

The Spirit and the Law

"If you are led by the Spirit you are not under the law." Galatians 5:18. "We know that the law is spiritual; but I am carnal, sold under sin." Romans 7:14. The flesh and the spirit are in opposition; but against the fruits of the Spirit "there is no law." Galatians 5:22, 23. Therefore the law is against the works of the flesh. The carnal mind is "not subject to the law of God." So those who are in the flesh cannot please God but are "under the law." This is another clear proof of the fact that to be "under the law" is to be a transgressor of it. "The law is spiritual." Therefore all who are led by the Spirit are in full harmony with the law, and so they are not *under* it.

Here again we see that the controversy was not whether or not the law should be kept, but *how* it could be fulfilled. The Galatians were being led astray by the flattering teaching that they themselves had power to do it, while the heaven-sent apostle strenuously maintained that only through the Spirit could it be kept. This he showed from the Scriptures, from the history of Abraham, and from the experience of the Galatians themselves. They began in the Spirit, and as long as they continued in the Spirit, they ran well. But when they substituted themselves for the Spirit, immediately works began to manifest themselves which were wholly contrary to the law.

The Holy Spirit is the life of God; God is love; love is the fulfilling of the law; the law is spiritual. Therefore whoever would be spiritual must submit to the righteousness of God which is "witnessed" to by the law but is gained only through the faith of Jesus Christ. Whoever is led by the Spirit must keep the law, not as a condition of receiving the Spirit but as the necessary result.

We often find people who profess to be so spiritual, so wholly led by the Spirit, that they do not need to keep the law. They admit that they do not keep the law, but say that it is the Spirit that leads them to do as they do. Therefore, they reason, it cannot be sin, even though opposed to the law. Such make the terrible mistake of substituting their own carnal mind for the mind of the Spirit. They have confounded the flesh with the Spirit and have thus put themselves in the place of God. To speak against the law of God is to speak against the Spirit. They are terribly blinded and should pray, "Open my eyes, that I may behold wondrous things out of Thy law." Psalm 119:18.

²² But the fruit of the Spirit is love, joy, peace, patience, kindness, goodness, faith, ²³ gentleness, self-control; against such there is no law.

The first fruit of the Spirit is love, and "love is the fulfilling of the law." Joy and peace come next, for, "being justified by faith, we have peace with God through our Lord Jesus Christ. ... And not only so, but we also joy in God through our Lord Jesus Christ." Romans 5:1, 11, KJV. Christ was anointed with the Holy Spirit (Acts 10:38), or, as stated in another place, "with the oil of gladness" (Hebrews 1:9). The service of God is a joyful service. The kingdom of God is "righteousness and peace and joy in the Holy Spirit." Romans 14:17. He who is not glad in adversity as well as in prosperity does not yet know the Lord as he should. The words of Christ lead to fullness of joy. John 15:11.

Love, joy, peace, long-suffering, patience, kindness, goodness, faith, gentleness, self-control—these must come forth spontaneously from the heart of the true follower of Christ. They cannot be forced. But they do not dwell naturally in us. It is natural for us to be angry and exasperated instead of gentle and long-suffering when opposed. Note the contrast between the works of the flesh and the fruit of the Spirit. The first come naturally; therefore, in order for the good fruit to be born, we must be made completely over into new creatures. "The good man out of the good treasure of his heart produces good." Luke 6:45. Goodness comes not from any man, but from the Spirit of Christ continually dwelling in him.

²⁴ And those who belong to Christ Jesus have crucified the flesh with its passions and desires.

"Our old man is crucified with Him, that the body of sin might be destroyed, that henceforth we should not serve sin. For he that is dead is freed from sin." Romans 6:6, 7, KJV. "I am crucified with Christ; nevertheless I live; yet not I, but Christ liveth in me; and the life which I now live in the flesh I live by the faith of the Son of God, who loved me, and gave Himself for me." Galatians 2:20, KJV. This is the experience of every true child of God. "If anyone is in Christ, he is a new creature." 2 Corinthians 5:17. He still lives in the flesh, to all outward appearance the same as other men; yet he is in the Spirit and not in the flesh. Romans 8:9. He lives in the flesh a life that is not of the flesh, and the flesh has no power over him. But so far as its works are concerned, he is dead. "The body is dead because of sin; but the Spirit is life because of righteousness." Romans 8:10, KJV.

²⁵ If we live by the Spirit, let us also walk by the Spirit. ²⁶ Let us have no self-conceit, no provoking of one another, no envy of one another.

Is there any doubt here as to whether Paul believed Christians live in the Spirit? Not the slightest! No doubt is even implied! Because we live in the Spirit, we are in duty bound to submit to the Spirit. Only by the Spirit's power, the same Spirit that in the beginning hovered over the face of the deep and brought order out of chaos, can any person live. "The Spirit of God has made me, and the breath of the Almighty gives me life." Job 33:4. By the same breath were the heavens made. Psalm 33:6. The Spirit of God is the life of the universe. The Spirit is the universal presence of God, in whom "we live and move and have our being." Acts 17:28. We are dependent on the Spirit for life; therefore we should walk according to, or be guided by, the Spirit. This is our "reasonable service." Romans 12:1, 2.

What a wondrous life is here set forth! To live in the flesh as though the flesh were spirit. "There is a natural body, and there is a spiritual body. ... Howbeit that was not first which is spiritual, but that which is natural; and afterward that which is spiritual." 1 Corinthians 15:44, 46, KJV. The natural body we now have. The spiritual body all the true followers of Christ will receive at the resurrection. See 1 Corinthians 15:42-44, 50-53. Yet in this life, in the natural body, men are to be spiritual—to live just as they will in the future spiritual body. "You are not in the flesh, you are in the Spirit, if the Spirit of God really dwells in you." Romans 8:9.

"That which is born of the flesh is flesh, and that which is born of the Spirit is spirit." John 3:6. By our natural birth we inherit all the evils enumerated in this fifth chapter of Galatians, "and the like." We are fleshly. Corruption rules in us. By the new birth we inherit the fullness of God, being made "partakers of the divine nature, having escaped the corruption that is in the world through lust." 2 Peter 1:4, KJV. "The old man, which is corrupt according to the deceitful lusts" (Ephesians 4:22, KJV), is crucified, or put off, "that the body of sin might be destroyed, that henceforth we should not serve sin." Romans 6:6, KJV.

Abiding in the Spirit, walking in the Spirit, the flesh with its lusts has no more power over us than if we were actually dead and in our graves. It is, then, the Spirit of God alone that animates the body. The Spirit uses the flesh as an instrument of righteousness. The flesh is still corruptible, still full of lusts, still ready to rebel against the Spirit; but as long as we *yield our wills* to God, the Spirit holds the flesh in check. If we waver, if we in our hearts turn back to Egypt, or if we become self-confident and so relax our dependence on the Spirit, then we build again the things that we destroyed, and make ourselves transgressors. See Galatians 2:18. *But this need not be.* Christ has "power over all flesh," and He has demonstrated His ability to live a spiritual life in human flesh.

This is the Word made flesh. God manifest in the flesh. It is the revelation of "the love of Christ which surpasses knowledge, that you may be filled with all the fullness of God." Ephesians 3:19. With this Spirit of love and meekness ruling us, we will not be desirous of vainglory, provoking one another, envying one another. All things will be of God, and this will be acknowledged so that none will have any disposition to boast over another.

This Spirit of life in Christ—the life of Christ—is given freely to all. "Whosoever will, let him take the water of life freely." Revelation 22:17, KJV. "For the life was manifested, and we have seen it, and bear witness, and show unto you that eternal life, which was with the Father, and was manifested unto us." 1 John 1:2, KJV. "Thanks be to God for His inexpressible gift!" 2 Corinthians 9:15.

CHAPTER 6

The Glory of the Cross

Hasty readers are likely to think that there is a portion between chapters 5 and 6, and that the latter part treats of practical, spiritual life, while the first part is devoted to theoretical doctrines. This is a great error.

The object of this letter is clearly seen in this closing portion. It is not to furnish ground for controversy, but to silence it by leading the readers to submit themselves to the Spirit. Its purpose is to reclaim those who are sinning against God by trying to serve Him in their own weak way, and to lead them to serve indeed in newness of Spirit. All the so-called argument of the preceding portion of the letter is simply the demonstration of the fact that "the works of the flesh," which are sin, can be escaped only by the "circumcision" of the cross of Christ—by serving God in Spirit and having no confidence in the flesh.

¹ Brethren, if a man is overtaken in any trespass, you who are spiritual should restore him in a spirit of gentleness. Look to yourself, lest you too be tempted.

When men set out to make themselves righteous, pride, boasting, and criticism lead to open quarrels. So it was with the

Galatians, and so it will always be. It cannot be otherwise. Each individual has his own conception of the law. Having determined to be justified by the law, he reduces it to the level of his own mind so that *he* may be judge. He cannot resist examining his brethren, as well as himself, to see if they are up to his measure. If his critical eye detects one who is not walking according to his rule, he at once proceeds to deal with the offender. The self-righteous ones constitute themselves their brother's keeper to the extent of keeping him out of their company lest they should be defiled by contact with him. In marked contrast with this spirit, which is all too common in the church, is the exhortation with which this chapter opens. Instead of hunting for faults that we may condemn them, we are to hunt for sinners that we may save them.

To Cain, God said, "If you do well, will you not be accepted? And if you do not do well, sin is crouching at the door; its desire is for you, but you must master it." Genesis 4:7. Sin is a ravenous beast, lurking in secret, watching every opportunity to spring upon and overcome the unwary. Its desire is to us, but power has been given us to master it. "Let not sin therefore reign in your mortal bodies." Romans 6:12. Nevertheless it is possible (not necessary) for the most zealous ones to be overtaken. "I am writing this to you so that you may not sin; but if anyone does sin, we have an Advocate with the Father, Jesus Christ the righteous; and He is the expiation for our sins, and not for ours only but also for the sins of the whole world." 1 John 2:1, 2. So, even though one may stumble, he is to be restored and not thrust farther away.

The Lord represents His work by the case of the shepherd who seeks after the one sheep that has gone astray. The work of the gospel is an individual work. Even though under the preaching of the gospel thousands accept it in one day as the result of one discourse, the success is because of its effect on each individual heart. When the preacher in speaking to thousands addresses each one individually, he is doing the work of Christ. So if a man be overtaken in a fault, restore him in the spirit of meekness. No man's time is so precious that it is wasted when devoted to the salvation of one single person. Some of the most important and glorious truths that we have on record as uttered by Christ were addressed to only one listener. He who looks after and cares for the single lambs of the flock is a good shepherd.

"God was in Christ reconciling the world to Himself, not counting their trespasses against them, and entrusting to us the message of reconciliation." 2 Corinthians 5:19. "He Himself bore our sins in His body." 1 Peter 2:24. He did not impute our trespasses to us, but took them all on Himself. "A soft answer turns away wrath." Proverbs 15:1. Christ comes to us with gentle words, not harshly chiding us, in order that He may win us. He calls us to come to Him and find rest, to exchange our galling yoke of bondage and heavy burden for His easy yoke and light burden. Matthew 11:28-30.

All Christians are one in Christ, the Representative Man. Therefore "as He is so are we in this world." 1 John 4:17. Christ was in this world as an example of what men ought to be and of what His true followers will be when wholly consecrated to Him. To His disciples He says, "As the Father has sent Me, even so I send you." John 20:21. To this end He clothes them with His own power through the Spirit. "God sent the Son into the world, not to condemn the world, but that the world might be saved through Him." John 3:17. Therefore *we* are not sent to condemn, but to save. Hence the injunction, "If a man be overtaken in any trespass … restore him." This is not to be limited to those who are associated with us in church capacity. We are sent as ambassadors for Christ to beseech men to be reconciled to God. 2 Corinthians 5:20. No higher office can be found in heaven or earth than that of ambassador for Christ, which is also the office of even the lowliest and most despised soul that is reconciled to God.

"You Who Are Spiritual"

Only such ones are called upon to restore the erring. None others *can* do it. The Holy Spirit alone must speak through those who would reprove and rebuke. It is Christ's own work that is to be done, and only by the power of the Spirit can anybody be a witness to Him.

But would it then not be great presumption for anybody to go to restore a brother? Would it not be as much as claiming that he himself is spiritual?

It is indeed no light matter to stand in Christ's place to any fallen man. The design of God is that each one should take heed to himself: "Look to yourself, lest you too be tempted." The rule here laid down is calculated to work a revival in the church. As soon as a man is overtaken in a fault, the duty of each one is not straightway to talk to somebody about him, nor even to go directly to the erring one himself, but to ask himself, "How do *I* stand? Am I not guilty, if not of the same thing, of something equally bad? May it not even be that some fault in me has led to his fall? Am I walking in the spirit, so that I could restore him and not drive him farther away?" This would result in a complete reformation in the church, and it might well be that by the time the others had got into condition to go to the faulty one he might also have recovered himself from the snare of the devil.

In giving directions how to deal with one who has committed a trespass (Matthew 18:5-18), the Saviour said, "Truly, I say to you, whatever you bind on earth shall be bound in heaven, and whatever you loose on earth shall be loosed in heaven." Verse 18. Does this mean that God pledges Himself to be bound by any decision that any company of men calling themselves His church may make? Certainly not. Nothing that is done on earth can change God's will. The history of the church as we have it for nearly two thousand years is a record of mistakes and errors, of self-aggrandizement and of putting self in the place of God.

What, then, did Christ mean? He meant just what He said. His instruction shows that He meant that the church should be spiritual, filled with the spirit of meekness, and that everyone who spoke should "speak as the oracles of God." Only the word of Christ should be in the heart and mouth of all who deal with a trespasser. When this is the case, it follows (since God's word is settled forever in heaven) that whatever is bound on earth must necessarily be bound in heaven. But this will not be the case unless the Scriptures are strictly followed in letter and in spirit.

² **Bear one another's burdens, and so fulfil the law of Christ.**

"The law of Christ" is fulfilled by bearing one another's burdens, because the law of Christ's life is to bear burdens. "Surely He has borne our griefs and carried our sorrows." Whoever would fulfill His law must still do the same work for the strayed and fallen.

"In all things it behooved Him to be made like unto His brethren. ... For in that He Himself hath suffered being tempted,

He is able to succor them that are tempted." Hebrews 2:17, 18, KJV. He knows what it is to be sorely tempted, and He knows how to overcome. Although He "knew no sin," He was made even to be sin for us that we might be made the righteousness of God in Him." 2 Corinthians 5:21. He took every one of our sins and confessed them before God as His own.

Even so He comes to us. Instead of upbraiding us for our sin, He opens His heart to us and tells us how He has suffered with the same hardship, pain, sorrow and shame. Thus He wins our confidence. Knowing that He has passed through the same experience, that He has been down to the very depths, we are ready to listen to Him when He talks about the way of escape. We know that He is talking from experience.

The greatest part therefore of the work of saving sinners is to show ourselves one with them. It is in the confession of our own faults that we save others. The man who feels himself without sin is not the man to restore the sinful. If you say to one who is overtaken in any trespass, "How in the world could you ever do such a thing? I never did a thing like that in my life! I can't see how anybody with any sense of self-respect could do so," you might far better stay at home. God chose one Pharisee, and *only* one, to be an apostle. And he was not sent forth until he could acknowledge himself to be the chief of sinners.

It is humiliating to confess sin, but the way of salvation is the way of the cross. It was only by the cross that Christ could be the Saviour of sinners. Therefore, if we would share His joy, we must with Him endure the cross, despising the shame. Remember this fact: It is only by confessing our own sins that we can save others from their sins. Only thus can we show them the way of salvation; for it is he who confesses his sins that obtains cleansing from them and so can lead others to the fountain.

³ For if any one thinks he is something, when he is nothing, he deceives himself. ⁴ But let each one test his own work, and then his reason to boast will be in himself alone and not in his neighbor.

Mark those words, "when he is nothing." It does not say that we should not think ourselves to be something until we are something. No; it is a statement of the fact that we *are* nothing. Not merely a single individual but all nations are nothing before the Lord. If we ever at any time think ourselves to be something, we deceive ourselves. And we often do deceive ourselves and thus mar the work of the Lord.

Remember "the law of Christ." Although He was everything, He "emptied Himself" that the work of God might be done. "A servant is not greater than his master." John 13:16. God alone is great. "Every man at his best state is altogether vanity." Psalm 39:5, KJV. God alone is true but every man a liar. When we acknowledge this and live in consciousness of it, we are where the Spirit of God can fill us, and then God can work through us. The "man of sin" is he who exalts himself. 2 Thessalonians 2:3, 4. The child of God is the one who humbles himself.

⁵ For each man will have to bear his own load.

Is this a contradiction of Verse 2? By no means. When the Scripture tells us to bear one another's burdens, it does not tell us to throw our burdens on one another. Each one is to cast his burden on the Lord. Psalm 55:22. He bears the burden of all mankind, not en masse, but for each one individually. We don't cast our burdens on Him by gathering them up in our hands or with our mind and hurling them from ourselves to one who is at a distance. That can never be done. Many have tried to get rid of their burden of sin and pain and care and sorrow but have failed. They have felt it roll back upon their own heads heavier than ever until they have almost sunk in despair. What was the trouble? Simply this: They regarded Christ as at a distance from them, and they felt that they themselves must bridge the gulf. It is impossible. The man who is "without strength" cannot cast his burden the length of his arm. As long as we keep the Lord at arm's length, we do not know rest from the weary load. It is when we recognize and confess Him as our sole support, our life, the One whose power it is that makes every motion, and so confess that we are nothing and sink out of sight, that we leave the burden resting on Christ. He knows what to do with it. And yoking up with Him, we learn from Him how to bear the burdens of others.

Then how about bearing our own burden? It is the divine "power that worketh in us" that bears it! "I am crucified with Christ: nevertheless I live; yet not I, but Christ liveth in me." Galatians 2:20, KJV. It is I, and yet it is not I, but Christ.

Now I have learned the secret! I will not weary someone else with the story of my burden but will bear it myself; yet not I, but Christ in me. There are people enough in the world who have not yet learned this lesson of Christ so that every child of God will always find work to do in bearing burdens for others. His own he will entrust to the Lord. Is it not wonderful to have "One who is mighty" always carrying our burden?

This lesson we learn from the life of Christ. He went about doing good because God was with Him. He comforted the mourners. He bound up the brokenhearted, He healed all that were oppressed of the devil. Not one who came to Him with a tale of sorrow or distressing malady was turned away without relief. "This was to fulfill what was spoken by the prophet Isaiah, 'He took our infirmities and bore our diseases.'" Matthew 8:17.

And then when night sent the multitude to their beds, He sought the mountain or the forest, that in communion with the Father, by whom He lived, He might find a fresh supply of life and strength for His own soul. "Let each one test his own work." "Examine yourselves, to see whether you are holding to your faith. Test yourselves. Do you not realize that Jesus Christ is in you?—unless indeed you fail to meet the test!" 2 Corinthians 13:5. "He was crucified in weakness, but lives by the power of God. For we are weak in Him, but in dealing with you we shall live with Him by the power of God." Verse 4. So if our faith proves to us that Christ is in us (and faith proves to us the reality of the fact) we have rejoicing in ourselves alone, and not in another. We joy in God through our Lord Jesus Christ, and our joy does not depend upon any other person in the world. Though all should fail and be discouraged, we can stand, for "God's firm foundation"—Christ—"stands." 2 Timothy 2:19.

Therefore let no one who calls himself a Christian be content to lean on somebody else. Let him, though he be the weakest of the weak, be a burden bearer, a worker together with God, in Christ bearing quietly and uncomplainingly his own burdens and those of his neighbors also. He can discover some of the burdens of his uncomplaining brother and bear them, and the other will do likewise. So the rejoicing of the weak will be, "The Lord God is my strength and my song, and He has become my salvation." Isaiah 12:2.

[6] Let him who is taught the Word share all good things with him who teaches.

There can be no doubt that this refers primarily to temporal support. If a man gives himself wholly to the ministry of the Word, it is evident that the things necessary for his maintenance must come from those who are taught. But this by no means exhausts the meaning of the injunction. The one who is taught in the Word must share with the teacher "all good things." Mutual help is the burden of this chapter. "Bear one another's burdens." Even the teacher who is supported by those who are taught is to use his money to assist others. Christ and the apostles, who had nothing of their own—for Christ was the poorest of the poor, and the disciples had left all to follow Him—nevertheless distributed to the poor out of their little store. See John 13:29.

When the disciples told Jesus to send the hungry multitudes away that they might buy themselves food, He said, "They need not go away; you give them something to eat." Matthew 14:16. He was not trifling with them. He meant what He said. He knew that they had nothing to give the people, but *they had as much as He had.* They did not see the power of His words, so He Himself took the few loaves and dealt out to the disciples, and thus they really did feed the hungry people. But His words to them meant that they should do just what He did. How many times our own lack of faith in Christ's word has hindered us from doing good and sharing what we have (Hebrews 13:16), the sacrifices which please God.

As the teachers share not only the Word but give temporal support as well, so those who are taught in the Word should not confine their liberality merely to temporal things. It is a mistake to suppose that ministers of the gospel never stand in need of spiritual refreshment or that they cannot receive it from the weakest in the flock. No one can ever tell how much the souls of teachers are encouraged by the testimonies of faith and joy in the Lord which come from the mouths of those who have heard the Word. It is not simply that the teacher sees that his labor is not in vain. The testimony may have no reference whatever to anything that he has done. But a humble soul's joyful testimony to what God has done for him will often, through the refreshment it gives the teacher of the Word, be the means of strengthening the souls of hundreds.

7 Do not be deceived; God is not mocked, for whatever a man sows, that he will also reap. 8 For he who sows to his own flesh will from the

flesh reap corruption; but he who sows to the Spirit will from the Spirit reap eternal life.

This is a simple statement of fact that cannot be made plainer by any amount of talk. The harvest, which is the end of the world, will reveal whether the sowing has been wheat or tares. "Sow to yourselves in righteousness, reap in mercy; break up your fallow ground: for it is time to seek the Lord, till He come and rain righteousness upon you." Hosea 10:12, KJV. "He that trusteth in his own heart is a fool" (Proverbs 28:26, KJV); and equally foolish is he who trusts in other men, as is seen from verse 13 of Hosea 10. "Ye have plowed wickedness, ye have reaped iniquity; ye have eaten the fruit of lies; because thou didst trust in thy way, in the multitude of thy mighty men." "Cursed be the man that trusteth in man, and maketh flesh his arm," whether it be his own flesh or that of some other man. "Blessed is the man that trusteth in the Lord, and whose hope the Lord is." Jeremiah 17:5, 7, KJV.

Everything enduring comes from the Spirit. The flesh is corrupt and it corrupts. He who consults only his own pleasure, fulfilling the desires of the flesh and of the mind, will reap a harvest of corruption and death. But "the Spirit is life because of righteousness" (Romans 8:10, KJV), and he who consults only the mind of the Spirit will reap everlasting glory. "For if you live according to the flesh you will die, but if by the Spirit you put to death the deeds of the body you will live." Romans 8:13. Wonderful! If we live, we die; if we die, we live! This is the testimony of Jesus: "Whoever would save his life will lose it, and whoever loses his life for My sake will find it." Matthew 16:25.

This does not mean the loss of all joy in the present. It does not mean undergoing a continual deprivation and penance, going without something that we long for for the sake of getting something else by and by. It does not mean that life in this present time shall be a living death, a long-drawn-out agony. Far from it. That is a crude and false idea of the Christian life, the life that is found in death. No; whoever comes to Christ and drinks of the Spirit has in himself "a spring of water welling up to eternal life." John 4:14. The joy of eternity is his now. His joy is full day by day. He is abundantly satisfied with the "fatness of God's house," drinking of the river of God's own pleasure. He has all that he longs for, because his heart and his flesh cry out only for

God in whom is all fullness. Once he thought he was "seeing life," but now he knows that he was then but gazing into the grave, the pit of corruption. Now he begins really to live, and the joy of the new life is "unspeakable, and full of glory." So he sings:—

> "Now none but Christ can satisfy,
>   None other name for me;
> There's love, and life, and lasting joy,
>   Lord Jesus, found in Thee."

A shrewd general always seeks to seize upon the strongest positions. So wherever there is a rich promise to believers, Satan tries to distort it so as to make it a source of discouragement. Accordingly, he has made many believe that the words, "He who sows to his own flesh will from the flesh reap corruption," mean that they must all their lives, even after being born of the Spirit, suffer the consequences of their former life of sin. Some have supposed that even in eternity they would have to bear the scars of their old sins, saying, "I can never hope to be what I should have been if I had never sinned."

What a libel on God's mercy and redemption in Christ Jesus! That is not the freedom with which Christ makes us free. The exhortation is: "Just as you once yielded your members to impurity and to greater and greater iniquity, so now yield your members to righteousness for sanctification." Romans 6:19. But if the one who thus yields himself to righteousness must always be handicapped by his former bad habits, that would prove that the power of righteousness is less than that of sin. But God's grace is as mighty as the heavens.

Here is a man who for gross crimes has been condemned to imprisonment for life. After a few years' imprisonment he receives a free pardon and is set at liberty. Some time afterward we meet him and see a fifty-pound cannonball attached to his leg by a huge chain so that he can move about only with the greatest difficulty. "Why, how is this?" we ask in surprise. "Were you not given your freedom?"

"Oh, yes," he replies, "I am free; but I have to wear this ball and chain as a reminder of my former crimes."

Every prayer inspired by the Holy Spirit is a promise of God. One of the most gracious of these is this: "Remember not the sins of my youth, or my transgressions, according to Thy steadfast love remember me, for Thy goodness' sake, O Lord!" Psalm 25:7.

When God forgives and forgets our sins, He gives us such power to escape from them that we shall be as though we had never sinned. By the "exceeding great and precious promises" we are made "partakers of the divine nature, having escaped the corruption that is in the world through lust." 2 Peter 1:4, KJV. Man fell by partaking of the tree of knowledge of good and evil. The gospel presents such a redemption from the fall that all the black memories of sin are erased. The redeemed ones come to know only the good, like Christ, "who knew no sin."

They that sow to the flesh will from the flesh reap corruption, as we have all proved in ourselves. "But you are not in the flesh, you are in the Spirit, if the Spirit of God really dwells in you." Romans 8:9. The Spirit has power to free us from the sins of the flesh and from all their consequences. Christ "loved the church, and gave Himself for it; that He might sanctify and cleanse it with the washing of water by the Word, that He might present it to Himself a glorious church, not having spot, or wrinkle, or any such thing; but that it should be holy and without blemish." Ephesians 5:25-27, KJV. "With His stripes we are healed." The memory of sin, not of individual sins, will live in eternity only in the scars in the hands and feet and side of Christ. These are the seal of our perfect redemption.

⁹ **And let us not grow weary in well-doing, for in due season we shall reap, if we do not lose heart.**

It is so easy for us to get tired doing good when we are not looking to Jesus. We like to have little intermissions because constant doing good seems too much of a strain. But that is only when we have not fully learned the joy of the Lord, the strength that enables us to keep from getting weary. "They who wait for the Lord shall renew their strength, they shall mount up with wings like eagles, they shall run and not be weary, they shall walk and not faint." Isaiah 40:31.

But that which is especially referred to here, as the context shows, is not simply the resisting of temptation in our own flesh but the helping of others. Here we need to learn a lesson from Christ, who "will not fail or be discouraged till He has established justice in the earth." Isaiah 42:4. Though many whom He relieved never showed the least sign of appreciation, it made no difference with Him. He came to do good and not to be appreciated. Therefore, "in the morning sow your seed, and at evening withhold not your hand; for you do not know which will prosper, this or that, or whether both alike will be good." Ecclesiastes 11:6.

We cannot tell how much we will reap, nor from which of the seed that we sow. Some may fall by the wayside and be snatched away before it has time to take root; other may fall on stony ground where it will wither, and still other may fall among thorns and be choked. But one thing is certain, and that is that we shall reap. We do not know whether the morning sowing or the evening sowing will prosper, or whether both alike will be good; but there is no possibility that both can be bad. One or the other alone may prosper, or else both may be good.

Isn't that encouragement enough for us not to be weary in well-doing? The ground may seem poor, and the season may not be favorable. The prospect for a crop may be most unpromising, and we may be tempted to think that all our labor is wasted. Not so! "In due season we shall reap, if we do not lose heart." "Therefore, my beloved brethren, be ye steadfast, unmovable, always abounding in the work of the Lord, forasmuch as ye know that your labor is not in vain in the Lord." 1 Corinthians 15:58, KJV.

[10] So then, as we have opportunity, let us do good to all men, and especially to those who are of the household of faith.

In this we see that the apostle speaks of temporal help, for we need no special command to preach the Word to those who are not of the household of faith. They are the ones to whom it is especially to be preached. But there is a natural tendency—natural, I say, not spiritual—to limit charities to those who are called "deserving." We hear much about "the worthy poor." But we are all unworthy of the least of God's blessings; yet He showers them upon us continually. "If ye do good to them which do good to you, what thank have ye? For sinners also do even the same. And if ye lend to them of whom ye hope to receive, what thank have ye? For sinners also lend to sinners, to receive as much again. But love ye your enemies, and do good, and lend, hoping for nothing again; and your reward shall be great, and ye shall be the children of the Highest; for He is kind unto the unthankful and to the evil." Luke 6:33-35, KJV.

Doing good to others is to be considered a privilege to be

enjoyed and not an irksome duty to be discharged. Men do not speak of disagreeable things as opportunities. No one says that he had an opportunity to lose some money. On the contrary, a man will speak of an opportunity to make some money or to escape from some threatened danger. It is thus that we are to consider doing good to the needy.

But opportunities are always sought for. Men are always on the lookout for an opportunity to get gain. So the apostle teaches us that we should be *seeking* opportunities to help someone. This Christ did. He "went about doing good." He traveled about the country on foot, searching for opportunities to do somebody some good, and He found them. He did good, "for God was with Him." His name is Immanuel, which means "God with us." Now, as He is with us all the days even to the end of the world, so God is with us, doing good to us, that we also may do good.

¹¹ See with what large letters I am writing to you with my own hand.

The consuming zeal of the apostle Paul in writing is seen in the fact that, contrary to his usual custom, he seized the pen and wrote the letter, or part of the letter, with his own hand. As intimated in chapter 4, the apostle suffered from weak eyes. This hindered him much in his work, or would have hindered him but for the power of God resting on him. It was necessary for him always to have someone with him to minister to him. Some took advantage of this fact to write letters to the churches in Paul's name, which troubled the brethren. See 2 Thessalonians 2:2. But in 2 Thessalonians Paul showed them how they might know an epistle that came from him. No matter who wrote the body of it, he wrote the salutation and the signature with his own hand. So great was the urgency in this case, however, that he may have written the entire letter himself.

¹² It is those who want to make a good showing in the flesh that would compel you to be circumcised, and only in order that they may not be persecuted for the cross of Christ.

We cannot deceive God, and it is useless to deceive ourselves or others. "The Lord sees not as man sees; man looks on the outward appearance, but the Lord looks on the heart." 1 Samuel 16:7. The circumcision in which the "false brethren" were seeking to persuade the Galatians to trust meant self-righteousness instead of righteousness by faith. They had the law only as "the form of righteousness and of truth." With their works they could make "a good showing in the flesh," but it was only an empty show; there was no reality in it. They could seem righteous without suffering persecution for the cross of Christ.

¹³ For even those who receive circumcision do not themselves keep the law, but they desire to have you circumcised that they may glory in your flesh.

They did not indeed keep the law—not by any means. The flesh is opposed to the law of the Spirit, and "they that are in the flesh cannot please God." But they desired converts to "our faith," as so many call the particular theories which they hold. Christ said, "Woe unto you, scribes and Pharisees, hypocrites! For ye compass sea and land to make one proselyte, and when he is made, ye make him twofold more the child of hell than yourselves." Matthew 23:15, KJV. Such teachers glory in the flesh of their "converts." If they can count so many as belonging to "our denomination," so much "gain" in the past year, they feel virtuously happy. Numbers and appearances count for much with men but for nothing with God.

¹⁴ But far be it from me to glory except in the cross of our Lord Jesus Christ, by which the world has been crucified to me, and I to the world.

Why glory in the cross? Because by it the world is crucified to us and we to the world. The letter ends where it begins, with deliverance from "this present evil world." It is the cross alone that accomplishes the deliverance. The cross is the symbol of humiliation. Therefore we glory in it.

God Revealed in the Cross

"Let not the wise man glory in his wisdom, let not the mighty man glory in his might, let not the rich man glory in his riches." Jeremiah 9:23.

Why should not the wise man glory in his wisdom? Because so far as it is his own wisdom it is foolishness. "The wisdom of this world is folly with God." 1 Corinthians 3:19. No man has any wisdom in which to glory, for his own wisdom is foolishness. Wisdom which God gives is something to cause humility instead of pride.

What about might? "All flesh is grass." Isaiah 40:6. "Every

man at his best state is altogether vanity." Psalm 39:5, KJV. "Men of low degree are vanity, and men of high degree are a lie; to be laid in the balance, they are altogether lighter then vanity." But "power belongeth unto God." Psalm 62:9, 11, KJV.

As to riches, they are "uncertain." 1 Timothy 6:17. Man "heapeth up riches, and knoweth not who shall gather them." Psalm 39:6, KJV. "Riches certainly make themselves wings; they fly away as an eagle toward heaven." Proverbs 23:5, KJV. Only in Christ are found unsearchable and abiding riches.

Man therefore has absolutely nothing in which to boast. What is there left of a man when he has nothing that can be called wealth, no wisdom whatever, and absolutely no strength? Everything that man is or has comes from the Lord. Therefore it is that he that glories is to glory in the Lord. 1 Corinthians 1:31.

Now put this text with Galatians 6:14. The same Spirit inspired them both, so there is no contradiction. One text says that we are to glory only in the knowledge of the Lord. The other says that there is nothing in which to glory save the cross of our Lord Jesus Christ. The conclusion, therefore, is that in the cross we find the knowledge of God. To know God is eternal life, and there is no life for mankind except through the cross of Christ. So again we see most clearly that all that may be known of God is revealed in the cross. Aside from the cross, there is no knowledge of God.

This shows us again that the cross is seen in all creation. The everlasting power and divinity of God, all that may be known of Him, are seen in the things that He has made. Out of weakness God brings strength. He saves men by death, so that even the dead may rest in hope. No man can be so poor, so weak and sinful, so degraded and despised, that he may not glory in the cross. The cross takes him just where he is, for it is the symbol of shame and degradation. It reveals the power of God in him, and herein is ground for everlasting glory.

The Cross Crucifies

The cross cuts us off from the world. Glory! for then it unites us to God, because the friendship of the world is enmity with God. "Therefore whoever wishes to be a friend of the world makes himself an enemy of God." James 4:4. Through His cross Christ has destroyed the enmity. Ephesians 2:15, 16. "And the world passes away, and the lust of it; but he who does the will of God abides forever." 1 John 2:17. Then let the world pass away.

> "Fade, fade, each earthly joy.
> Jesus is mine;
> Break every tender tie,
> Jesus is mine.
> Dark is the wilderness;
> Earth has no resting place;
> Jesus alone can bless;
> Jesus is mine."

Jesus said, "I, when I am lifted up from the earth, will draw all men to Myself." John 12:32. This He said signifying what death He should die, namely, the death of the cross. "He humbled Himself" to death, "even death on a cross. Therefore God has highly exalted Him and bestowed on Him the name which is above every name." Philippians 2:8, 9.

It was through death that He ascended to the right hand of the Majesty in the heavens. It was the cross that lifted Him up from earth to heaven. Therefore it is the cross alone that brings us glory, and so it is the only thing in which to glory. The cross, which means derision and shame from the world, lifts us away from this world and sets us with Christ in the heavenly places. The power by which it does this is "the power that worketh in us," the power that works in and upholds all things in the universe.

[15] For neither circumcision counts for anything, nor uncircumcision, but a new creation.

Salvation does not come from man, whatever his state or condition, or whatever he may do. In an uncircumcised state he is lost. If he be circumcised, he is no nearer salvation. Only the cross has power to save. The only thing that is of any value is a new creature, or, as indicated in the Revised Standard Version, "a new creation." "If anyone is in Christ, he is a new creation" (2 Corinthians 5:17); and it is only through death that we become joined to Him. See Romans 6:3.

> "Nothing in my hand I bring;
> Simply to Thy cross I cling."

The cross makes a new creation. Here again we see a reason

for glorying in it. When the new creation came from the hand of God in the beginning, "the morning stars sang together, and all the sons of God shouted for joy." Job 38:7.

The Sign of the Cross

Put together all the texts that we have read: (1) The cross of Christ is the only thing in which to glory, (2) whoever glories must glory only in the knowledge of God, (3) God has chosen the weak things of the world to confound the mighty, so that none might glory save in Him, and (4) God is revealed in the things that He has made. Creation, which manifests God's power, also presents the cross, because the cross of Christ is the power of God and God is made known by it.

What have we? This: That the power it took to create the world and all things that are in it, the power that keeps all things in existence, is the power that saves those who trust in it. This is the power of the cross.

So the power of the cross, by which alone salvation comes is the power that creates and continues to work in all creation. But when God creates a thing it is "very good." So in Christ, in His cross, there is "a new creation." We are His workmanship, created in Christ Jesus for good works, which God prepared beforehand, that we should walk in them." Ephesians 2:10. It is in the cross that this new creation is wrought, for its power is the power by which "in the beginning God created the heavens and the earth." This is the power that keeps the earth from utter destruction under the curse, the power which brings about the changing seasons, seed time and harvest, and that will at last renew the face of the earth. "It shall blossom abundantly, and rejoice with joy and singing. The glory of Lebanon shall be given to it, the majesty of Carmel and Sharon. They shall see the glory of the Lord, the majesty of our God." Isaiah 35:2.

"The works of the Lord are great, sought out of all them that have pleasure therein. His work is honorable and glorious: and His righteousness endureth forever. He hath made His wonderful works to be remembered; the Lord is gracious and full of compassion." Psalm 111:2-4, KJV.

Here we see that the wonderful works of God reveal His righteousness, and His grace and compassion as well. This is another evidence that His works reveal the cross of Christ in which infinite love and mercy are centered.

But "He hath made His wonderful works to be remembered"; or, "He hath made a memorial for His wonderful works." Why does He wish men to remember and declare His mighty acts? In order that they may not forget but may trust in His salvation. He would have men continually meditate on His works so they can know the power of the cross. So when God had made the heavens and earth and all their host in six days, "on the seventh day God finished His work which He had done, and He rested on the seventh day from all His work which He had done. So God blessed the seventh day and hallowed it, because on it God rested from all His work which He had done in creation." Genesis 2:2, 3.

The cross conveys to us the knowledge of God because it shows us His power as Creator. Through the cross we are crucified to the world and the world to us. By the cross we are sanctified. Sanctification is the work of God, not of man. Only His divine power can accomplish the great work. In the beginning God sanctified the Sabbath as the crown of His creative work, the evidence that His work was finished, the seal of perfection. Therefore He says, "Moreover I gave them My Sabbaths, to be a sign between Me and them, that they might know that I the Lord sanctify them." Ezekiel 20:12.

So we see that the Sabbath, the seventh day, is the true sign of the cross. It is the memorial of creation, and redemption is creation, creation through the cross. In the cross we find the complete and perfect works of God and we are clothed with them. Crucified with Christ means the utter giving up of self, acknowledging that we are nothing, and trusting absolutely in Christ. In Him we rest. In Him we find Sabbath. The cross takes us back to the beginning into "that which was from the beginning." The resting upon the seventh day of the week is but the sign of the fact that in the perfect work of God, as seen in creation, in the cross, we find rest from sin.

The cross means death, but it also means the entrance into life. There is healing in Christ's wounds, blessing in the curse that He bore, life in the death that He suffered. Who dare say that he trusts Christ for everlasting life if he dare not trust Him for a few years or months or days of life in this world?

Now say once more, and say it from the heart: "Far be it from me to glory except in the cross of our Lord Jesus Christ, by which the world has been crucified to me, and I to the world." If you can say that in truth, you will find tribulations and afflictions so easy that you can glory in them.

The Glory of the Cross

It is by the cross that everything is sustained. "In Him all things hold together," and He does not exist in any other form than that of the crucified One. But for the cross there would be universal death. Not a man could breathe, not a plant could grow, not a ray of light could shine from heaven if it were not for the cross.

Now "the heavens declare the glory of God; and the firmament showeth His handiwork." Psalm 19:1, KJV. They are some of the things that God has made. No pen can describe and no artist's brush can depict the wondrous glory of the heaven. Yet that glory is but the glory of the cross of Christ. This follows from the facts already learned, that the power of God is seen in the things that are made, and that the cross is the power of God.

The glory of God is His power, for "the immeasurable greatness of His power in us" is seen in the resurrection of Jesus Christ from the dead. Ephesians 1:19, 20. "Christ was raised from the dead by the glory of the Father." Romans 6:4. It was for the suffering of death that Jesus was crowned with glory and honor. Hebrews 2:9.

So we see that all the glory of the innumerable stars, with their various colors, all the glory of the rainbow, the glory of the clouds gilded by the setting sun, the glory of the sea and of blooming fields and green meadows, the glory of the springtime and of the ripened harvest, the glory of the opening bud and the perfect fruit, all the glory that Christ has in heaven, as well as the glory that will be revealed in His saints when they "will shine as the sun in the kingdom of their Father" (Matthew 13:43), is the glory of the cross. How can we ever think of glorying in anything else?

[16] Peace and mercy be upon all who walk by this rule, upon the Israel of God.

The rule of glory! What a grand rule to walk by! Are there two classes mentioned? No, that cannot be, for the letter has been devoted to showing that all are one in Christ Jesus.

"We are the true circumcision, who worship God in spirit, and glory in Christ Jesus, and put no confidence in the flesh." Philippians 3:3. This circumcision constitutes us *all* the true Israel of God, for this is the victory over sin, and "Israel" means an overcomer. No longer are we "aliens from the commonwealth of Israel," "no more strangers and foreigners, but fellow citizens with the saints, and of the household of God; and are built upon the foundation of the apostles and prophets, Jesus Christ Himself being the Chief Cornerstone." Ephesians 2:12, 19, 20, KJV. So we shall join the throng that "will come from east and west and sit at table with Abraham, Isaac, and Jacob, in the kingdom of heaven."

[17] **Henceforth let no man trouble me; for I bear on my body the marks of Jesus.**
[18] **The grace of our Lord Jesus Christ be with your spirit, brethren. Amen.**

The Greek word "marks" is the plural of "stigma," which we have incorporated into our own language. It signifies shame and disgrace even as of old it meant a mark branded into the body of a culprit or of a recaptured runaway slave to show to whom he belonged.

Such are the marks of the cross of Christ. The marks of the cross were upon Paul. He had been crucified with Christ, and He carried the nailprints. They were branded on his body. They marked him as the bondservant, the slave of the Lord Jesus. Let no one, then, interfere with him; he was not the servant of men. He owed allegiance to Christ alone, who had bought him. Let no one seek to get him to serve man or the flesh, because Jesus had branded him with His mark and he could serve no other. Moreover, let men beware how they sought to interfere with his liberty in Christ or how they treated him, for his Master would surely protect His own.

Do you have those marks? Then you may glory in them, for such boasting is not vain and will not make you vain.

What glory there is in the cross! All the glory of heaven is in that despised thing. Not in the figure of the cross, but in the cross itself. The world does not reckon it glory. But then it did not know the Son of God; and it does not know the Holy Spirit, because it cannot see Him. May God open our eyes to see the glory so that we may reckon things at their value. May we consent to be crucified with Christ that the cross may glorify us. In the cross of Christ there is salvation. In it is the power of God to keep us from falling, for it lifts us up from earth to heaven. In the cross there is the new creation which God Himself pronounces "very good." In it is all the glory of the Father and all the glory of the eternal ages. Therefore God forbid that we should glory save in the cross of our Lord Jesus Christ, by which the world is crucified to us, and we unto the world.

> "In the cross of Christ I glory,
>   Towering o'er the wrecks of time;
> All the light of sacred story
>   Gathers round its head sublime."

Therefore—

> "Since I, who was undone and lost,
>   Have pardon through His name and Word;
> Forbid it, then, that I should boast,
>   Save in the cross of Christ, my Lord."

> "Where'er I go, I'll tell the story
>   Of the cross, of the cross;
> In nothing else my soul shall glory,
>   Save the cross, save the cross;
> And this my constant theme shall be,
> Through time and in eternity,
> That Jesus tasted death for me,
>   On the cross, on the cross."